SILVER NOMAD

SILVER NOMAD

JOURNEYS
AND PLACES
TO DISCOVER
IN YOUR
RETIREMENT

Eric Chaline

First edition for the United States and Canada
published in 2005 by
Barron's Educational Series, Inc.

Copyright © 2005 Quid Publishing

All inquiries should be addressed to:
Barron's Educational Series, Inc.
250 Wireless Boulevard
Hauppauge, New York 11788
http://www.barronseduc.com

ISBN-13: 978-0-7641-5903-9
ISBN-10: 0-7641-5903-8

Library of Congress Catalog Card No. 2005925462

Conceived, designed and produced by
Quid Publishing Ltd
Level Four
Sheridan House
114 Western Road
Hove BN3 1DD
England
www.quidpublishing.com

Design: Lindsey Johns
Illustrations: Matt Pagett

Printed and bound in China by Regent Publishing Services Ltd.

NOTE
The author, publisher and copyright holder assume no
responsibility for any injury, loss or damage caused or
sustained as a consequence of the use and application of
the contents of this book.

Travel broadens the mind, but it also invigorates the spirit and warms the heart and sinews, keeping you younger, and making you healthier and hopefully a little wiser too.

C O N T

Introduction 8

✳ SECTION ONE ✳
ROMANTIC LIAISONS

From Russia with Love 16
La Dolce Vita 20
Monsoon Romance 25
River of Dreaming Spires 28

✳ SECTION TWO ✳
ACTIVE BREAKS

Walking on the Wild Side 34
Going Dutch 38
The Land that Time Forgot 42
On Dracula's Trail 46
Giants of the Deep 50

✳ SECTION FIVE ✳
SPIRITUAL RETREATS

A Passage to Kerala 88
Singing the Land 92
The Enchanted Land 96
The Mountain of Heaven 100

✳ SECTION SIX ✳
GASTRONOMIC GETAWAYS

The World's Best Medicine 106
Feasting in the Land of Smiles 110
The Middle Way to Health 114
A Feast for the Spirit 118

E N T S

* SECTION THREE *

OFF-TRACK ADVENTURE

A Journey to Middle Earth 56

Lost Cities of the Jungle 60

The Call of the Wild 64

Kingdoms of the South 68

* SECTION FOUR *

CITIES OF CULTURE

The World's Stage 74

Island of the Bull 78

A Little Night Music 82

* SECTION SEVEN *

CONSUMER PARADISE

Golden Touch 124

Shopping à la Mode 128

Eastern Promises 132

Turkish Delights 136

References
and Resources 140

Experience Index 143

Introduction

When I started globe-trotting many years ago, the world, travelers, and travel were very different. Many of the destinations featured in this book were unknown or accessible only to the most adventurous and hardiest of backpackers; and "older" travelers were expected to stick to sedate winter vacations in Hawaii and Florida, restful cruises, or tours of Europe's capitals on which they were escorted by guides who interpreted places, peoples, and cultures for their benefit.

The "silver nomads" of the twenty-first century, who lend their name to the present volume, are a very different breed. Despite their years, they are more youthful, more hardy, and more adventurous; less inclined to follow the group tours and itineraries of preplanned vacations; more open to the new, the unknown, and the unexpected; they do not believe that adventure, activity, and romance are the province of the young.

The present volume is divided into seven sections, covering different types of travel: romantic, active, adventurous, cultural, spiritual, gastronomic, and consumer. However, within each recommended trip, you will find a range of options, so that even in an adventure break, you can find a cultural, romantic, or gastronomic option. An "Experience Index" at the end of the book will enable you to plan the trip, or trips, of a lifetime.

Whether it's relaxation, adventure, or culture, the "Experience Index" will allow you to plan the trip of a lifetime.

Even the seasoned silver nomad may find something of value in the following pages, which cover all the practical aspects of travel for the older traveler. In these times when health and security are of paramount importance, much of this section will be devoted to these topics, but you will also find tips on packing, exercise for long journeys, and ways of staying in touch with the folks back home.

HEALTH MATTERS

Medical services in North America, the European Union, Australia, New Zealand, and Japan are of an extremely high standard. Any medical emergency will be dealt with quickly and efficiently; the system for minor ailments will vary from country to country, but in most cases you will usually be expected to pay up front for a consultation and any necessary treatment, which will then be reimbursed by your insurance company upon your return. Make sure you obtain full medical reports and bills.

In the developing world, the best medical facilities are usually private. You could ask your insurance company if they have a list of recommended doctors and clinics in the area you are traveling to; if this is not available, you could call your consulate or embassy if you require routine medical treatment; or ask for a recommendation from a major international hotel in the vicinity. They will usually be able to recommend an English-speaking doctor.

Travel Insurance Few travelers will need to be told that they should take appropriate travel insurance, but when buying your policy, make sure that it covers the areas you plan to visit, the activities you intend to take part in, any special equipment you are taking with you, as well as the full duration of your trip. For example, many standard policies will cover only a 30-day trip, and may exclude certain areas and any special equipment. Some policies may have exclusions for preexisting medical conditions, so declare any serious conditions to ensure coverage for emergency treatment and the replacement of lost medication.

Immunizations Vaccinations are an important consideration when traveling to many areas of the world. A comprehensive list of the vaccinations required by region can be found at the World Health Organization Web site (www.who.int). A vaccination to consider wherever you are going is Hepatitis A, a water-borne disease that can affect you even in the developed world. Remember that most vaccinations have a limited duration, so make sure you keep yours up to date.

Malaria Malaria is a serious disease prevalent in low-lying tropical areas. There is currently no vaccination against malaria, and people traveling to areas where the malaria parasite mosquito is present need to take a course of a prophylactic drug such as chloroquine, both before and during your trip. No treatment is 100 percent effective, however, so wearing insect repellent, using a plug-in insect zapper, and sleeping under a mosquito net is advisable in high-risk areas.

Medication Get your doctor to give you a list of any medication you are taking, with both the brand name and the full chemical name of the drug, as the same drug can be called something different overseas. Make a copy of any prescriptions or list of medications and store it with copies of your other documents (see next section).

SECURITY

Documents Although the replacement of lost or stolen documents will be covered by your insurance policy, you will save a lot of time, frustration, and phone calls by making photocopies of documents such as passports, visas, airline tickets, insurance certificates, credit cards, travelers' checks' serial numbers, etc., and storing them separately from your actual documents.

Carrying money and documents safely Although a money belt is a very secure option, it is not always practical or comfortable; a document pouch worn on a strap around the neck that can be worn under clothes is a more comfortable alternative to a money belt, as is the ubiquitous "fanny pack." A shoulder bag with a zip fastener that can be slung over the head and shoulder is much more difficult to snatch than a handbag. Never carry documents in the outer pockets of knapsacks or backpacks.

Financial matters Carry an emergency amount in travelers' checks in US dollars (I usually take US$500), and keep them separate from your cash and credit cards. Be aware of the possibility of credit card or debit card fraud in shops and restaurants and at automated cash machines. In many countries, it will be safer to use cash, but carry only as much cash as you need for your outing and leave the rest in a hotel or room safe.

A secure way to carry and store your documents is a primary concern for travelers.

LUGGAGE AND PACKING

Every traveler will have his or her preference when it comes to luggage and packing. For years, I traveled with a canvas knapsack, which ensured that I only packed as much as I could carry (literally). However, in later years, when not hiking, I have favored the wheeled suitcase with extensible handle. Pick a model that will fit in the overhead compartment of a long-haul jet, and make sure the handle is fully adjustable. There is nothing worse than having a handle that is either too long or short. I prefer soft- to hard-body models, for lightness and expandability. If your case is not fitted with locks, purchase your own. A small padlock will not deter the determined thief but it will discourage an opportunist who might be tempted by an unlocked suitcase in a hotel room or airport storage area. Carry several waterproof containers for medication, electronic equipment, documents, and any product that might spill or leak during a trip.

Limiting the size of your luggage will force you to think about what you really need for your trip. Inexperienced travelers often pack far more than they will ever use, as well as many items that are not suited to their destination. Check out outdoor and camping stores for lightweight, foldaway, multipurpose clothing, in materials that do not need ironing, are easy to clean, and quick drying, so you can always look neat.

Convenient and easy to transport, the wheeled suitcase with an extendable handle is a good luggage option.

HEALTH AND FITNESS ON LONG TRIPS

Food and drink Recent research has confirmed what many seasoned travelers have known for a long time—alcohol, caffeine, and flying do not mix well. While a glass or two of wine with dinner will not do you any harm, avoid spirits, and make sure you keep well hydrated with liberal supplies of water.

Avoiding alcohol and caffeine and following an exercise routine will help you enjoy a lengthy flight.

Exercises on long journeys The recent concern about Deep Vein Thrombosis (DVT), the incidence of blood clots in the legs during long trips, make it advisable for all passengers to do some exercise on flights and bus and car rides over five to six hours. While it may be possible to stop and stretch your legs at regular intervals when you are driving, walking around the cabin is not always possible on a crowded airplane. To maintain good circulation, do the following exercises every one to two hours.

NECK CIRCLES: Rotate the head slowly but do not tilt it back to avoid neck strain. Repeat 5 times in each direction.

SHOULDER SHRUGS: Shrug the shoulders and rotate them 5 times to the back, and then 5 times to the front.

HANDLE GRIPS: With your forearms on the armrests, push down hard 5 times, holding the push for a few breaths.

KNEE PRESSES: With your hands pushing down on your thighs, push up with your feet 5 times, holding the push for a few breaths.

ANKLE STRETCHES: Stretch your legs, and press the footrest with your toes (feet extended) 5 times, and with your ankles (feet flexed) 5 times, holding each press for a few breaths.

ANKLE CIRCLES: Stretch your legs and rotate the ankles in both directions five times each.

SENIOR DISCOUNTS

Most countries in the developed world operate a range of national and local senior citizen discount plans. The rules vary from country to country, so to make sure you are not missing out, it is best to ask whether a discount is available. Remember that you may be asked for proof of age to qualify for the discount. In the developing world, senior citizen discounts are less common, and may be available only to the citizens of that country.

KEEPING IN TOUCH WITH THE FOLKS BACK HOME

Cell phones (known as mobile phones in the U.K.) provide the easiest means of keeping in touch. Your phone provider may offer an international roaming system so that you can use your phone overseas. However, this is usually an expensive option, especially if you are using a North American phone on a European network or vice-versa. A cheaper alternative is to buy a local network "pay-as-you-go" SIM card, which you can use in your handset during your vacation. If your phone is electronically locked, however, you can rent complete cell phones at most airports. On trips lasting several months, it may be cheaper to buy a local "pay-as-you-go" phone, which you can reuse on future trips to the same country.

International dialing cards are widely available and are an expensive alternative to using a cell phone.

E-mail is ideal for routine communications and to send and store digital pictures of your trip. Most Internet cafés now offer a picture-download facility. If you do not have an Internet account of your own, you can create an e-mail address quickly and easily (and for free) by opening a hotmail account (www.hotmail.com).

Messages in a bottle are no longer the only way to keep in touch with loved ones.

Lovers will take romance with them wherever the go, but some places in the world also have the power to inspire it.

ROMANTIC LIAISONS

The world is full of romantic possibilities—whether for a second honeymoon or for that trip you have been promising yourselves now that the kids have grown up and left home. Here are just a few suggestions that have enthralled lovers throughout the ages: a midnight train ride through the snow-hushed landscapes of Russia; strolls through the Renaissance cities of northern Italy; an unforgettable trip to India to gaze at an emperor's marble tear; and the discovery of the riverside castles that the kings of France built for love.

From Russia with Love

MIDNIGHT EXPRESS TO ST. PETERSBURG

From the heart of the new Russia's capital, you board the midnight express bound for far northern shores to the city of St. Peter, the "Venice of the North," a neoclassical marvel of majestic tree-lined vistas and canals, of golden-domed cathedrals, opulent palaces, and colonnaded piazzas.

WHERE

Men and women tightly wrapped in furs, their breath condensing in the night air, embrace on the platform. It is almost midnight. The guard announces the departure, the doors slam, and you settle back in the luxurious warmth of your first-class compartment. You have entered another age of travel, before the frantic bustle of airports and the sterile convenience of jumbo jets. The attendant serves your freshly brewed tea from a samovar as the Red Arrow Express pulls out of Moscow's Leningrad Station. The name takes you back to an earlier Russian era, of stark Soviet fervor expressed by the station's modernist architecture, but you are traveling even further back into Russia's past, to the imperial city of St. Petersburg on the shores of the Baltic Sea. Founded in 1712 by Czar Peter the Great at the mouth of the Neva River, it was to intended to be Russia's new capital and a window to the West. St. Petersburg remains Russia's very own City of Lights and city of romance.

LOCAL KNOWLEDGE

The daily Red Arrow Express from Moscow's Leningradsky Vokzal (Leningrad Station) departs punctually at five minutes to midnight. You will need to reserve your seats at least one day in

St. Petersburg was founded by Czar Peter the Great in 1712 to showcase Russian achievements in art, architecture, and technology.

advance or earlier at busy times (see Reference Section, p.142 for further information). A two-berth first-class compartment will provide you with all the necessary comfort and privacy, but to travel in style, a VIP compartment with two beds and a private bathroom is also available. Your attendant will serve you tea and biscuits, but should you want to enjoy a midnight supper or cocktail, you will have to make your own arrangements. The train arrives at the Moskovsky Vokzal (Moscow Station) in St. Petersburg at eight o'clock the following morning.

WHEN TO VISIT

St. Petersburg is a year-round destination suitable for lovers of cold and temperate climates. While midsummer temperatures rarely exceed a comfortable 68°F (20°C), midwinter temperatures can drop to a chilly 5°F (-15°C). The city's proximity to the Arctic Circle means long summer days and long winter nights. The St. Petersburg year is marked by seasonal festivals and events; the endless days of summer, when darkness never falls, are enlivened by the White Nights Festival of opera and ballet; an international classical music festival is held in April and May, and the winter festival takes place from December 25 to January 5. Late February heralds the End of Winter Festival, with sleigh rides and other snow activities.

"A silent lonely beauty"
Lillian Hellman on St. Petersburg in
An Unfinished Woman, 1969

WHAT TO DO

✳ Take a stroll arm-in-arm along St. Petersburg's Champs-Elysées, Nevsky Prospekt, which runs 2 miles (4 km) through the heart of the city from the classical splendor of the Admiralty to the riverside Alexander Nevsky Monastery. Thronged with strollers and shoppers both summer and winter, Nevsky Prospekt is lined with Art Déco and Art Nouveau department stores, boutiques, cafés, bars, and restaurants, and several of the city's major landmarks, including the colonnaded Our Lady of Kazan Cathedral, a miniature version of St. Peter's Basilica in Rome, and the Stroganov and Beloselksy-Belozersky palaces.

✳ Attend an enchanted gala night of music at the Mariinsky (formerly Kirov) Theater during the month-long White Nights Festival, and then enjoy a princely candle-lit supper at the Dviranskoye Gnezdo (Nobleman's Nest) on the grounds of the former palace of the Yusupov family.

✳ Along with the Metropolitan in New York, the Louvre in Paris, and the National Gallery in London, the State Hermitage Museum, housed in the rococo splendor of the Winter Palace, ranks among the world's most extraordinary art collections. But the Hermitage is only one of the cultural landmarks of the city. Two other museums of note are the

Museum of Decorative and Applied Arts, featuring rooms decorated in past historical styles, and the Russian Museum in the Mikhailovsky Palace.

＊ To get a sense of the elegance of nineteenth-century St. Petersburg, visit the city's oldest park between Mars Field and the Fontanka River. Laid out by Peter the Great with fountains, pavilions, and formal gardens to resemble an eighteenth-century European park, it was the place of choice for the gentry to promenade in pre-Revolutionary days. While in the park, take a moment to visit the small Summer Palace, which was Peter the Great's first official residence in the city.

＊ Board the hydrofoil at the Winter Palace riverside and sail along the Neva River to the Gulf of Finland where Peter the Great laid out his grandest residences at Petrodvorets (formerly Peterhof). The 300-acre park contains 66 fountains and 12 miles (19 km) of canals, which culminate in the unforgettable Grand Cascade and Water Avenue. Among the many palaces, pavilions, and summerhouses on the grounds, Peter's favorite residence, Mon Plaisir, has bright, airy rooms overlooking the sea. The Grand Palace was enlarged for Czarina Elizabeth and remodeled for Catherine the Great.

＊ More intimate than Petrodvorets are the summer palaces of Tsarkoe Selo (renamed Pushkin in 1937 to commemorate the centenary of the poet's death) built for the czarinas Elizabeth and Catherine the Great 16 miles (26 km) south of the city. The blue and white façade of the Catherine Palace glitters with golden domes. No less luxurious are the exquisite interiors of the palace, which was the last residence of the tragic imperial couple, Nicholas and Alexandra.

The Grand Cascade is the glory of Petrodvorets.

19

La Dolce Vita

Embark on a tour of northern Italy's most romantic cities: Venice, home of the original "carnevale;" Sienna, with the color and pageantry of the annual "palio" horse races; Florence, city of art and architecture; and Verona, famed for the opera festival staged in its Roman arena.

"The gorgeous and wonderful reality of Venice is beyond the fancy of the wildest dreamer. Opium couldn't build such a place, and enchantment couldn't shadow it in a vision."
Charles Dickens, 1844

WHERE

If you had to pick one region of the world that could provide everything a vacationer desires: unequaled scenery, a unique architectural and cultural heritage, a warm, welcoming people, and delicious food and wine, it would have to be northern Italy. During the cultural and artistic flowering of the Renaissance between the thirteenth and sixteenth centuries, the northern half of the Italian peninsula was a patchwork of independent city-states competing with one another in the fields of banking, trade, and industry, art and architecture, and often in war. This sense of a local identity and loyalty to the city of one's birth has survived into the later centuries of Italian unity and modernity. The brightest stars of the Renaissance pantheon are the cities north of Rome; the undisputed artistic capital of Italy, Florence, or Firenze to the Italians, is the principle city of Tuscany; neighboring Pisa is famed for its architectural oddity, the "Leaning Tower;" Sienna, is the city of pageantry, with the excitement of horse races run through the city center; Verona, the home of Shakespeare's star-crossed lovers, Romeo and Juliet, boasts a vast Roman amphitheater; and, of course, the unforgettable city of romance, Venice.

The architectural treasures of Italy's Renaissance cities, Florence, Sienna, Venice, and Pisa, have been lovingly and faithfully restored and preserved.

WHAT TO DO

* The water-bound city of Venice is unforgettable in its own right, but during its annual themed carnival, or *Carnevale*, it becomes still more extraordinary. Held every year in the ten days before Shrove Tuesday (last week of January—first week of February), the *Carnevale* is an extravaganza of processions, galas, theatrical entertainments, cocktail parties, and balls, all held in fancy dress in the piazzas and palazzos of the city. Not to be missed is the *Ballo del Doge*, the Doge's Ball, named for the ancient ruler of the city.

* Verona, 71 miles (114 km) west of Venice has two claims to fame, one ancient, the other modern. It is to a story told in old Verona that Shakespeare owes his *Tragedy of Romeo and Juliet*, and today you can visit the fourteenth-century palazzo from whose balcony Juliet declaimed, "Romeo, Romeo, wherefore art thou, Romeo?"
As great a draw to the city, is the summer-long opera festival held in the 2,000-year-old Roman Arena di Verona, an acoustically perfect venue set in the beautiful Veneto countryside. One of the most popular performances, and therefore one for which you will have to book well in advance, is Verdi's ancient-Egyptian operatic extravaganza, *Aïda*.

* Florence, the capital of Tuscany, is so rich in treasures that the first-time visitor is at a loss to know where to start. Step into any church or *palazzo* and you will encounter masterworks of the Renaissance: a fresco by da Vinci, an altarpiece by Raphael, a sculpture by Michelangelo. But these wonders are only ornaments for the greatest treasure of all, which is the city itself. Florence is always a popular destination, so avoid it in midsummer, when it is too hot

and crowded. Discover it on a warm jasmine-scented June evening, when the busloads of tourists have left, the Florentines are enjoying their evening meal, and the city is briefly your own.

✳ Less than an hour's drive from Florence, the city of Pisa is known throughout the world for its famous "Leaning Tower," designed to be the bell tower for the neighboring twelfth-century cathedral. The tower, whose deviation from verticality began soon after its completion, finally threatened to topple altogether. Now entirely restored and with its foundations reinforced, the tower reopened for guided visits in 2001.

✳ Held in the Piazza del Campo, the historic heart of the city of Sienna, 21 miles (34 km) south of Florence, the *palio* horse races take place twice every summer on July 2 and August 16. Do not be deceived: the 1,000-meter race is not just a procession but is run for real. Its very real thrills and spills will have you on the edge of your seat, cheering loudly for your chosen team. The winning horse, with or without rider, wins honor for his sponsors and a banner depicting the Virgin Mary.

✳ Another ten or so miles south of Florence, you will catch sight of the hill town of San Gimignano, a medieval Manhattan, which once had more than 70 slender watchtowers soaring into the Tuscan sky as confidently as any modern-day skyscraper. Today, only fourteen survive, and those open to the public offer you an unrivaled view of the surrounding Chianti wine-producing region. Busy during the day with thousands of tourists, the walled town recovers its tranquility in the late afternoon. Arrive late or stay the night in one of the town's inexpensive *pensiones* or small hotels.

WHEN TO VISIT

Like much of Western Europe, the northern Italian year is divided into four well-defined seasons. Summers are warm to hot, with plenty of beach and sunbathing weather. However, July and August are also the peak vacation months, and you will find the sites crowded with local and overseas tourists. Being a peninsula, Italy benefits from mild winters, but the downside is that it can be wet and foggy in fall and winter. Much the best time to visit is in late spring-early summer (May and June) and late summer-early fall (September and October), when the temperatures are pleasantly temperate and the sites less crowded.

Like some magnificent and impossibly ornate passenger liner, the city of Venice floats on the waters of the Lido, its inhabitants sailors on the sea of time.

The Taj Mahal in Agra is so familiar that is has become a visual cliché, but no other building in the world will suprise and delight you more when you visit it for the very first time.

Monsoon Romance

Contemplate the world's most beautiful memorial to love by moonlight, and then ride on the "Palace on Wheels" through the regal cities of Rajasthan, where you can sample life in a maharajah's palace built in the center of a lake.

WHERE

The Mughal rulers of India built Agra on the banks of the Yamuna River to be the capital of their empire. Even after the capital was moved 123 miles (198 km) to the northeast to Delhi, the city remained an important military, religious, and commercial center, as shown by the many important Mughal buildings and shrines in the city and its environs. The most important, and a building so iconic that just a glimpse of its marble dome and four slender minarets immediately transport the viewer to the Indian subcontinent, is the Taj Mahal, tomb and shrine to the enduring devotion of one man for his lost love. Not far from Agra, stands the hauntingly beautiful city of Fatehpur Sikri, abandoned only twenty years after its founding. Traveling further south, you enter the desert kingdoms of the Rajputs in the province of Rajasthan. This warrior people retained their ancient rulers—known as rajahs—even when India came under British dominion, and the region is dotted with their extravagant palaces and fantastic capital cities.

LOCAL KNOWLEDGE

The two-hour air-conditioned ride on the Taj Express from Delhi to Agra is much more comfortable and picturesque than the four-hour journey by car or bus. Agra has been on the tourist trail ever since the Taj Mahal was built, so if you have not booked an all-inclusive tour, be prepared to be assailed by guides and rickshaw peddlers when you arrive and to be "diverted" on your way to one of the many souvenir and gift shops selling the full range of Indian goods and the semiprecious stones that the

WHAT TO DO

∗ The Taj Mahal, although it has long been one of the world's photographic icons, will not disappoint. I first saw it during a monsoon, its fragile white dome etched against an ink-black sky by jagged lighting bolts. But rain or shine, as you step through the gateway, you will savor that moment of recognition. Once you are walking through the gardens, your viewpoint of the Taj and its scale changes, and when you finally reach it, it is transformed once more. Every inch of the pristine whiteness you glimpsed from afar is inlaid with elaborate floral designs executed in semiprecious stones.

∗ If you were suddenly dropped in Fatehpur Sikri, a short drive from Agra, you might think that a magician had woven a spell and taken you back in time. Abandoned a mere twenty years after its founding in 1571, the palaces, temples, and mosques of Fatehpur Sikri were built in red sandstone in the high Mughal style combining Arab, Persian, and Indian architecture.

∗ Combining twenty-first-century convenience with nineteenth-century opulence, the "Palace on Wheels" train gives the visitor the taste of how the Rajput maharajahs once traveled across their domains. Operating from September to April, the train departs from New Delhi and stops at all the major sites of historical and natural interest in Rajasthan.

∗ A major stop on the "Palace on Wheels" itinerary is Jaipur, the capital of Rajasthan, also known as the "Pink City" because of the ocher-pink color of its buildings and city walls. The most stunning of the city's many monuments is the five-story Hawa Mahal, the Palace of the Winds.

region produces and that were used extensively to decorate the Taj Mahal. Allow yourself to make one of these impromptu stops but then insist on being taken straight to the Taj. Since 2004 the Taj is open for nighttime visits, but you will need to book as places are limited.

WHEN TO VISIT

In general, the best time of year to visit India is between March and October. However, the one period of the year when it is not advisable to visit Agra is during the monsoon season, which occurs from mid-July to mid-August. This does not apply to Rajasthan, which is an area of arid deserts and is at its coolest in the monsoon months.

"You cannot keep your enthusiasms down, you cannot keep your emotions within bounds as that soaring bubble of marble breaks into view." Mark Twain on seeing the Taj Mahal

* Take a camel trek across the desert around the fortress of Jaisalmer in western Rajasthan. Founded in the twelfth century as a staging post between India and Central Asia, Jaisalmer is a walled city built in golden sandstone.

* Without a doubt the most romantic city in India, Udaipur overlooks the tranquil waters of Lake Pichola. In addition to the vast City Palace, ornamented with a multitude of balconies, towers, and cupolas, the city boasts of two other palaces built on islands in the center of the lake: the Jag Niwas and Jag Mandir. The maharana of Udaipur's summer palace, the Jag Niwas, is now the luxury Lake Palace Hotel, where you can sample the lifestyle of a Rajput prince.

* The months of October and November witness an important festival in Puskhar, 75 miles (120 km) from Jaipur. This yearly event combines a religious pilgrimage to the sacred Lake Pushkar, a cattle and camel fair, markets for handicrafts, as well as camel races and circuses.

For romance Mughal style, stay at the Jag Niwas Palace Hotel, which is built in the center of Lake Pichola.

SHAH JAHAN AND MUMTAZ MAHAL

Love matches were rare in the seventeenth century, as much in the East as they were in the West, but that such a union should take place between the Emperor of India, Shah Jahan, and his Persian bride, Princess Arjumand Banu, is worthy to be included among *The Tales of 1,001 Nights*. Married at 20 and 19 respectively, Shah Jahan and Arjumand, remembered by history as Mumtaz Mahal ("Exalted One of the Palace"), lived happily until Mumtaz's death nineteen years later. The heartbroken emperor pledged to build his wife a memorial that would withstand the ages. It took 20,000 craftsmen 22 years (1631–1653) to complete this exquisite memorial that floats serenely above the waters of the ornamental pools of its gardens.

River of Dreaming Spires

CASTLES OF THE VAL DE LOIRE

Step back in time to the courtly world of sixteenth-century France. Built by the kings of France for their queens and mistresses, the "chateaux" of the Loire Valley are the jewels of Renaissance architecture. Follow in the footsteps of royal ladies in sumptuous pleasure gardens, and dine on the region's famed "cuisine gastronomique."

WHERE

The Loire Valley draws a sweeping arc across the French heartland, from the Atlantic coast, through the ancient towns of Angers, Tours, Blois, and Orléans, to its source in the Massif Central mountains. The region's lush pastureland, rippling fields of corn, fruit-laden orchards, and productive vineyards make it France's food basket and the home of traditional French *gastronomie*. Set on the Loire's banks and on those of several of its confluents are the *chateaux* of the Loire, built between the fourteenth and the sixteenth centuries by the kings and princes of France. Unlike the forbidding fortresses of earlier times, the *chateaux* were not built for war or to withstand sieges. Designed in an era of peace and plenty, they are architectural extravaganzas of galleries, turrets, spires, and domes, set in exquisite formal gardens and pleasure parks—the models for the fairy-tale castles of *Beauty and the Beast* and *Sleeping Beauty*.

> *"One of the most wonderful rivers in the world, mirroring from sea to source a hundred cities and five hundred towers."*
> Oscar Wilde on the Loire

The currents of France's history, culture, and tradition flow with the same majesty as the Loire.

WINES OF THE VAL DE LOIRE

Although it cannot claim the *grand crues* vintage wines of the Bordeaux (see p.106) and Bourgogne regions, the Loire Valley is the home of some of France's most popular regional wines. Vineyards offer tours and tastings throughout the year. Try the wines of Mesland, between Amboise and Blois; Azay-le-Rideau is known for its white and rosé wines; Vouvray is a fruity wine with a light effervescence that makes it suitable for desserts or celebrations. Other vineyards worth a visit are Montlouis, between Amboise and Tours, and Chinon whose vines are grown on chalky terraces.

WHAT TO DO

The *chateaux* of the Loire Valley are accessible by car, bus, and bicycle, but an unusual way to see them and their ornate gardens is from the air; several companies offer flights by hot air balloon, helicopter, and small aircraft over the region's main castles and towns.

∗ Amboise

Acknowledged to be the birthplace of the French Renaissance style, the *chateau* was built in the fifteenth century by the young King Charles VIII after a visit to the home of the style, Italy. It is in the nearby Manoir du Clos-Lucé that Leonardo da Vinci spent the last three years of his life as a guest of King Francis I. Throughout July and August, Amboise stages a spectacular *son et lumière* (sound and light show) with period costumes and horses, which features the famous historical figures who stayed at the castle.

∗ Azay-le-Rideau

The writer Balzac described the *chateau* at Azay-le-Rideau as a "Finely cut diamond whose facets are reflected in the River Indre." Built by the treasurer of France, Gilles Berthelot, the chateau was destined to remain unfinished, when Gilles provoked the king's anger and was forced to flee for his life.

∗ Blois

The city of Blois occupies a prime site on the Loire. King Louis XII began the building of its castle. However, it is the northwest wing with its Italian-style *loggias* built for Francis I that is the castle's glory.

∗ Chambord

The most famous and majestic of the *chateaux* of the Loire Valley, Chambord is a place of superlatives. Set in France's largest enclosed park, now a forest reserve, this castle will amaze visitors with its size, setting, furnishings, and architecture. One of its most unusual features is the double staircase attributed to Leonardo da Vinci. It is known as the "Stair of the Lost Lovers," because you might miss your beloved as she descends one flight to meet you, and you ascend by the other.

∗ Chaumont

The *chateau* overlooks the Loire River, standing amid tranquil gardens, and its austere design reminds the visitor of the original

THE FEAST OF SAINT JOAN

Every year on May 8th, the town of Orléans commemorates its rescue from the English by Joan of Arc in 1429. A young woman from the city is chosen to play Joan's part and lead the procession through the streets of the city, on horseback and dressed in full armor.

A statue of St. Joan, at Orléans.

The Chateau de Chenonceau was built for the love of two beautiful women, including Queen Marie de Medicis.

medieval fortress that once occupied the site. Among the highlights are the luxurious stables and a particularly fine collection of furniture, tapestries, and objets dating from the sixteenth to the nineteenth centuries.

✳ Chenonceau

Without a doubt Chenonceau is the most charming and romantic of all the *chateaux* of the region. Several royal ladies contributed to its construction. The most famous were the beautiful Diane de Poitiers, mistress of Henri II, and his queen, Marie de Medicis, who built the magnificent gallery across the River Cher.

✳ Cheverny

Although architecturally one of the most modern *chateaux* of the Loire Valley, the seventeenth-century Cheverny is also one of

the most luxurious. It is in the *Orangerie* that the *Mona Lisa* and many of France's most famous artworks found refuge during World War II. Its other claim to fame is to have served as the model for Captain Haddock's residence in the *Tintin* comic books.

✳ Langeais

In contrast to Cheverny, Langeais allows the visitor to step back into the late Middle Ages. Its fortifications are real and not for show, and the furnishings, tapestries, and huge fireplaces are all pure fifteenth century.

✳ Villandry

The glory of the Chateau de Villandry is its extraordinary Renaissance garden, which is unique in Western Europe. The *chateau* itself is a fine example of French Renaissance style.

WHEN TO VISIT

Central France has clearly marked seasons, with hot summers and cold winters, punctuated by mild springs and falls. To avoid the extremes of the climate and the vacation crowds, the best times to visit are late spring-early summer (May-June), when the gardens of the *chateaux* come to life, or in late summer-early fall (September-October), when the regions forests begin to take on their fall hues, and the annual *vendanges* (harvesting) takes place.

Long gone are the days when vacations meant spending time on a beach; today, the growth area is the activity break.

ACTIVE BREAKS

You have had your last family vacation looking out for the kids and sweating over what you have to do to keep them amused. Now you can pick and choose what you want to do. Here are a few ideas for the activity vacation of a lifetime. Discover the joys of nature photography in South Africa; captain your own barge on the waterways of Holland; go vampire hunting in the haunted Carpathian Mountains; visit the real "Jurassic Park" off the coast of Ecuador; or brave Arctic seas to pursue the giants of the deep.

Walking on the Wild Side

NATURE PHOTOGRAPHY IN SOUTH AFRICA

On a photography safari in South Africa's national parks and private game reserves, your everyday shots will be of lions at rest and play, grazing antelope and zebra, vast herds of wildebeests migrating across the veldt, and elephants and giraffes browsing among the upper branches of acacia trees.

WHERE

The Republic of South Africa is unrivaled for the range of its national parks and private game reserves that cover every type of natural environment, from the traditional African veldt, with the "big five" animals that people come to Africa to see—lions, leopards, elephants, buffaloes, and rhinos—in addition to huge herds of zebras, antelopes, and wildebeests; bird sanctuaries with some of the richest and most varied collections of birdlife on the planet; marine reserves where you can swim with dolphins and whale-watch; deserts, whose inhabitants still follow the age-old ways of their ancestors; and mountain wildernesses with breathtaking scenery. Local operators offer a huge range of tours, from the rugged trek across the *lowveldt* with nights spent under canvas, to the luxury of four-star lodges and safaris in air-conditioned landcruisers. Whichever you choose, you will not lack the opportunities to develop your photographic skills. Just make sure you pack enough film!

LOCAL KNOWLEDGE

Professional photographers recommend a 200mm telephoto lens when photographing wildlife, but many amateurs prefer the versatility of a zoom lens. And because you can often get quite close to the animals in the wild, a 35mm camera may also be of use. A solution is to take two cameras

Photo-safaris will enable you to capture some unforgettable wildlife images.

fitted with different lenses, so that you are always ready for a shot. Whichever lenses you pick, always protect them with filters, at minimum with a UV filter. When game viewing from a landcruiser, a steady platform for your camera is not always available. One solution is to use faster-than-normal film (with an ISO rating of 50 to 200); another, recommended by safari pros, is to rest your camera on a 5-pound (2.3 kg) bag of rice, securely wrapped and taped. A question is how much film to pack. A good figure to work on is about three rolls of 36 exposures per day, making an average of 20 rolls on a two-week safari. Film processing is best done on your return to your home country. Be aware that since 9/11 any film packed in checked luggage is likely to be seriously damaged or destroyed by the new security measures in use in most international airports. Take your film with you in your carry-on (both going and coming back),

storing it in a see-through plastic bag so it can easily be inspected. Also make sure that the carry-on X-ray machine is film safe.

WHEN TO VISIT

South Africa is in the Southern Hemisphere and its seasons are reversed from those of the North. Even in winter (July-September) the temperatures are extremely mild, except in the mountains where you may experience the occasional frost and snowfall. Summer (December-February) can be very hot and humid, especially along the northeastern coast. The eastern and western Cape provinces have a delightful climate, and gardeners will enjoy the springtime show of native wildflowers. South Africans are avid nature lovers and travelers themselves, so during the main school vacations (April, July, and September) the national parks and resorts are extremely busy with local as well as overseas visitors.

WHAT TO DO?

✳ As well as being one of the most famous and largest wildlife parks in the world, covering some two million hectares (five million acres), the Kruger National Park is also one of the oldest; it was set up in 1898 to preserve the *lowveldt* environment and its animals. The downside of the Kruger's fame, accessibility, and popularity is that it is crowded all year round.

✳ In order to enjoy the *lowveldt* without the crowds, check out the private game reserves on the western borders of the Kruger National Park, which offer safari lodge accommodations ranging in style (and price) from basic rusticity to unashamed four-star luxury.

✳ The region's largest national park, the Kgalagadi Transfrontier Park was created by the merger of South Africa's Kalahari-Gemsbok National Park and the Mabuasehabe-Gemsbok National Park in neighboring Botswana. The park is almost twice the size of the Kruger, and it is this enormous size that gives it its ecological importance, because herbivores, such as antelopes, are free to migrate great distances across to find food and water. The open terrain and sparse vegetation combine to create a natural photographic studio for grazing animals and their predators. The Kgalagadi is also famous for its birdlife, in particular its birds of prey.

✳ The awesome Drakensberg ("Dragon Mountains") are a basalt escarpment on the border of South Africa and Lesotho. A large part of the Drakensberg is taken up by national parks, the most spectacular of which is Royal Natal National Park. The park's main feature is the Amphitheatre, a rock wall 3 miles (5 km) in length, and averaging

South Africa's national parks and private game reserves present a variety of options for the nature photographer.

Southern Africa's natural wonders are not limited to the four-legged variety. The region is famous for its awesome scenery, which provides opportunities for landscape photographers.

¾ of a mile (1,000 m) in height. Another feature is the Tugela Falls, whose upper reaches sometimes freeze in winter forming a dazzling column of ice.

* Perhaps one of the best-known geographical features anywhere in the world, Table Mountain, which overlooks the city of Cape Town, is also a unique micro ecosystem featuring some unusual fauna and flora, including South Africa's national flower, the protea, and the cute, inquisitive dassie, or mountain hyrax. If you don't like the thought of the arduous climb on foot, you can always take the ten-minute ride by cable car. Some 38 miles (60 km) from Cape Town is Cape Point, which is also preserved as a national park.

* The Wilderness National Park, in the heart of South Africa's Garden Route, offers captivating landscapes of lakes, rivers, estuaries, and beaches, set against a backdrop of lush vegetation and lofty mountains.

Going Dutch

SAILING THE DUTCH WATERWAYS

Explore Holland's verdant and flower-filled countryside along its unrivaled network of rivers and canals. As master of your own vessel, or as a passenger on a luxury crewed boat, you will sail below the slowly turning sails of windmills and find yourself suddenly amid the riotous color of the world's largest tulip fields.

WHERE

The kingdom of The Netherlands is rightly known as the "garden of Europe." Not only is it the home of hundreds of varieties of tulips, the nation's floral emblem, but its giant flower fields have also long supplied most of Europe's bulb and cut flower markets. Canals and rivers crisscross the country's famously flat landscapes, which are dotted with windmills and picturesque villages. Once the arteries of commerce, they now provide the visitor with the most pleasant and relaxing way to see Holland's ancient cities, flower fields, and parks. You can choose from large four- and five-star passenger vessels equipped with cabins, private bathrooms, gourmet restaurants, and spa

An example of Holland's trademark architecture.

facilities, or rent your own flat-bottomed barge, a crewed fishing ship, schooner, or yacht to cruise the canals at your own pace.

WHAT TO DO

* Whatever your budget and level of sailing experience, you will be able to find a formula that suits you on the Dutch waterways. Once of the most popular options is to rent your own fully restored historic flat-bottomed barge, which provides the comfort and facilities of a vacation apartment with the mobility and freedom of a camper van.

* Between March and May the 32-hectare (80-acre) Keukenhof Gardens situated just outside the town of Lisse, south of Haarlem, burst into life with stunning floral displays of breathtaking beauty. Millions of tulips and other bulbs emerge from winter hibernation, giving the visitor a multicolored spectacle to photograph.

* The Rijnland area, situated on the west coast of Holland with its flower fields, beaches and dunes, small villages, and the historic city of Leiden, is a perfect introduction to Holland. The picturesque towns of Noordwijk and Katwilk combine dunes, forests, and miles of unspoiled sandy beaches with a lively resort atmosphere.

* Early birds will enjoy the world's largest flower auctions: the Aalsmeer (close to Amsterdam) and Flora Holland (close to Rotterdam or The Hague).

A very different kind of highway beckons in The Netherlands. On this "road trip" you may very well get your feet wet!

Visitors can view the millions of cut blooms that await shipment to Europe, North America, and Asia, and to attend the auctions, but be prepared to get there before the auctions start at 6 A.M.

* April to September is the flower parade or "corso" season. Although flower parades are not unique to Holland, it is here that they are the most numerous and the most spectacular. The season kicks off with the Bollenstreek (bulb-growing area) Flower Parade in April. Half a century ago, the organizers of the many small parades held in the villages and towns of the Bollenstreek decided to join forces and create one huge floral spectacle. The floats are decorated with an astounding 1.5 million hyacinths, as well as thousands of narcissi and other cut flowers.

Slow-turning windmill sails over fields of multicolored blooms typify the Dutch countryside in springtime.

LOCAL KNOWLEDGE

If you've never driven anything more challenging than the family sedan or an SUV, you might be concerned about sailing your own boat along rivers and canals. But neither previous experience nor a sailing license is required when renting a barge in Holland. The typical flat-bottom Dutch barge is easy to handle and slow, with an average cruising speed of 5–6.5 mph (8–10 km/h). The quiet waterways you will sail are mostly non tidal, with gentle currents, making them easy to navigate.

You are free to stop when and where you please, at a marina or in the open countryside. The plentiful moorings along the waterways are usually free of charge except for a few harbors in the most popular areas. One of the joys of canal cruising is going through locks. Many of these are operated for you by a lockkeeper, or open automatically as you approach, but others you have to operate yourself. They provide a great opportunity to meet the locals and other travelers. An average cruising day of four to

TULIPS

Scholars now believe that the emblematic Dutch tulip originated in the Caucasus region of eastern Europe and was first cultivated sometime in the eleventh century. The first European to mention the flowers was the Austrian ambassador to the Ottoman court of Constantinople (now Istanbul), who recorded seeing tulips in the Sultan's Topkapi Palace gardens in 1556. By the 1560s a few bulbs had begun to appear in Europe, and they soon became extremely sought after. The man responsible for introducing them to Holland was Carolus Clusius, who had been appointed head botanist at the University of Leiden in 1593. The flower was particularly well suited to the Dutch climate, and horticulturalists were soon competing to create ever more colorful varieties of tulips, such as the white and red *Semper Augustus*. The fascination with the flower sparked a speculative "tulip mania" in 1636–1637. In a seventeenth-century version of the "dot-com boom," investors gambled their entire fortunes on a single bulb that had not even flowered. As with all crazes, tulip mania came to a crashing end when the Dutch government moved to control the trade, leading to financial ruin for many speculators.

five hours will take you 18–25 miles (30–40 km), but remember to add on about 20 minutes for each lock you need to go through.

WHEN TO VISIT

The low-lying kingdom of The Netherlands benefits from a maritime climate. Winters are mild, but like fall, can be overcast, foggy, and wet. Summers are pleasantly warm without the heat of the inland regions of continental Europe. July and August are the busiest times for the major attractions, but the best time to sail in Holland is spring and early summer (April–June) when the many flower fields and parks of Holland burst into life.

The Land that Time Forgot

GALAPAGOS ISLANDS

Home of prehistoric iguanas and giant turtles, sea mammals, and some of the richest and most varied birdlife on earth, which gave Charles Darwin the clues to unlock the secrets of evolution, the Galapagos Islands are a fragile natural paradise that is a must-see for every ecotourist.

WHERE

The Galapagos are a unique treasury of marine, avian, and terrestrial life. Here you will be able to swim with green sea turtles, sea lions, and the world's only colony of equatorial penguins; scuba dive with manta rays and hammerhead sharks; wander among colonies of frigate birds and blue-footed boobies; and marvel at the land and marine iguanas, the descendants of the dinosaurs that ruled the earth 60 million years ago. The archipelago is spread over 19,500 square miles (50,000 km²) of the Pacific Ocean, 625 miles (1,000 km) west of the coast of the South American country of Ecuador, which administers the islands as a world heritage site and nature reserve. Comprising thirteen major islands, five of

which are inhabited, the archipelago is volcanic in origin. The highest point on the island chain is the 5,500-foot (1,707 m) Wolf Volcano on the island of Isabella, and the barren lava-strewn landscapes of the islands have an eerie, haunting beauty.

CHARLES DARWIN ON THE GALAPAGOS

Charles Darwin sailed for the Galapagos Islands on the HMS *Beagle* as a young man of 20 in 1831. The discoveries and observations that he made on the islands led to the development of the theory of evolution, which he set out in *The Origin of Species* (1859). It was the variety of species of Galapagos finches that gave Darwin important clues about the processes of natural selection that are the key to evolution. Although they were all descended from a common mainland ancestor, the Galapagos finches have developed into thirteen distinct species, each adapted to the environments and food supplies of the different islands of the archipelago.

Galapagos iguanas are distant descendants of the fearsome dinosaurs that ruled the earth 65 millions years ago. These monsters, however, are strictly vegetarian.

WHAT TO DO

∗ As you follow your naturalist guide across the hauntingly beautiful, alien volcanic landscapes of the Galapagos, you will discover the archipelago's unique flora and fauna, including giant land tortoises and land and sea iguanas. Thankfully, these fierce-looking descendants of T-Rex are vegetarians, feeding on cacti and algae. Another photogenic denizen of the seashore is the bright-red Sally Lightfoot crab, which fires salvos of seawater to vent its shell.

∗ The wealth of Galapagos birdlife is one of the main draws to the islands. A sight not to be missed is when the albatrosses gather in the thousands on the island of Isabela to court and breed every October. Another famous Galapagos regular, the male frigate bird, is easily identifiable during the mating season by the bright red air sack that it inflates to attract its mate.

∗ On walks through the islands' bird colonies you will observe the antics of the most famous Galapagos bird, the blue-footed booby. This strange bird so amused the first Spanish visitors to the island that they called them "*bobos*," the Spanish word for clown. Boobies court their mates by dancing on their outsized blue feet, honking and whistling as they point skyward with their beaks. They make guano nests on the ground, and like many of the local birdlife, are quite fearless of humans, so you

Unrivaled for its natural riches, the Galapagos offers wildlife explorations on land, in the skies, and under the sea.

will be able to get up close and personal with these "clowns" of the bird kingdom.

∗ The archipelago is the home of one of the rarest birds of prey in the world, the Galapagos hawk. As only 150 mating pairs remain, you will be extremely fortunate to catch sight of one of these soaring equatorial predators.

∗ The marine environment around the islands provides many unforgettable sights and experiences. You will need only a mask, snorkel, and flippers to swim with green sea turtles and among the world's only colonies of equatorial penguins, or frolic with inquisitive sea lions.

∗ The islands also offer unforgettable opportunities for scuba divers, such as diving with hammerhead sharks and manta rays off the uninhabited Wolf and Darwin islands.

∗ As most visitors to the Galapagos will travel via South American Ecuador, a good complement to your trip is a visit to the Ecuadorian Amazon rain forest. Here you can observe the native wildlife from treetop walkways, sail in dugout canoes on river and lake safaris, and meet the local Quechua Native American Indians.

The Galapagos's avian clown, the blue-footed booby.

WHEN TO VISIT

Sitting close to the Equator, the Galapagos are blessed with hot weather all year-round. There are slight climatic variations caused by changes in the trade winds and the Humboldt Current. June to December, when the water is cooler, is known as the "dry season," when sea mammals and seabirds are at their most active. The corresponding "warm season," which is more tropical and wetter, is from December to May. The low season months on the island are April-May and September-October, when you will find lower prices and a greater choice of accommodations and boats. To protect the fragile ecosystem of the islands, tourist numbers to the park are limited to around 60,000 a year. If you intend to travel to the islands during high season, be sure to book well in advance.

"I never dreamed that islands, about fifty or sixty miles apart, and most of them in sight of each other ... would have been so differently tenanted."
Charles Darwin

On Dracula's Trail

CARPATHIAN MOUNTAINS, ROMANIA

Although the author of "Dracula," Bram Stoker, portrayed Transylvania as a forbidding place haunted by the undead, the modern visitor will find spectacular scenery, romantic castles, historic towns and villages, and a wealth of wildlife on guided treks through the Carpathian Mountains of modern-day Romania.

"No country is kinder to the wanderer who has good legs."
Walter Starkie on Romania, 1933

WHERE

Home of the legendary Count Dracula, the Carpathian Mountains in the north Balkan republic of Romania are one of Europe's best-kept secrets. Like the much more famous Alps and Pyrenees of Western Europe, the Carpathians offer the visitor a wealth of activities, but without the crowds, and at a fraction of the cost. Summer provides opportunities for hiking through the area's many national parks, visits to health spas, and dips in crystal-clear glacial lakes; winter is a time for the full range of winter sports. Painted as a land of impenetrable forests haunted by vampires and werewolves, Transylvania is in reality a land of mountain peaks piercing blue skies above wooded valleys and sparkling streams; of charming villages with high-roofed wooden churches and richly decorated houses; of romantic castles perched on vertiginous mountaintops and historic walled cities. Tradition is still very much alive in Transylvania; villagers wear their colorful regional costumes on Sundays and for wedding celebrations and festivals, farmers travel around the country in horse-drawn carts, and shepherds sell tasty homemade cheeses by the roadside.

More fanciful than sinister, the lofty Bran Castle is one of the many places in the Carpathian Mountains associated with Vlad "the Impaler," aka, Count Dracula.

WHAT TO DO

* The medieval Saxon town of Brasov, 100 miles (160 km) north of the capital, Bucharest, is the gateway to the Transylvanian mountain country. Set amid the foothills of the Carpathians, it is one of Romania's most popular tourist destinations. The town's best-known landmark, the Black Church, said to be the largest Gothic church in Eastern Europe, owes its name to fire damage from 1689.

* The high Fagaras Mountain ridge, which runs for 50 miles (80 km) through the Transylvanian Carpathians, rarely dipping below 6,000 feet (2,000 m), offers some of the region's most spectacular hiking. As you follow the trail, you will pass below Romania's highest peak, Mt. Moldoveanu (8,480 feet/2,544 m), cross the highest highway in Europe, and skirt Romania's highest glacial lake, Lake Mioarele (7,484 feet/2,280 m). The Carpathians have a wealth of wildlife, including extremely rare populations of European bears and wolves.

* Bran Castle (founded 1377), popularly known as "Dracula's Castle," is 19 miles (30 km) south of Brasov. Despite the tourist-office hype, this castle has no proven links with the famous Vlad the Impaler, the fifteenth-century warrior on whose life Bram Stoker based his own creation, Count Dracula. More fanciful than sinister, this turreted, whitewashed fortress is not likely to inspire dread, even on the stormiest of nights.

* Far more sinister than Bran is Poienari Castle, over the border in the province of Wallachia, which you reach in an arduous climb of 1,500 steps. The now desolate, windswept ruin was a stronghold of Vlad the Impaler, and it is a far more fitting home for fiction's premier lord of the undead.

* The winter-sports resort of Sinaia in the Bucegi Mountains is known as the "Pearl of the Carpathians." Close by is royal Peles Castle (built 1873), an architectural extravaganza in the German Renaissance style.

* The city of Sighisoara is another medieval town with a Dracula connection. You can visit the house where Vlad the Impaler was born and spent his first years. The walled medieval town and its fortress are beautifully preserved, and are less crowded than the more popular Brasov.

* Sibiu, another medieval Saxon town, is famous for its pastel-colored houses painted in blues, oranges, and greens. The upper and lower town are linked by a warren of tunnels, stairways, and secret passages.

THE REAL DRACULA

Most people have heard of the world's most famous vampire, either from Bram Stoker's novel *Dracula* (1897), or the many Hollywood movies based on it. But who was the man behind the legend? Vlad "Tepes," Romanian for "the Impaler," (b. 1431) was a Wallachian ruler who resisted the invading Ottoman Turks. In his lifetime he was known as "Dracula," meaning "son of the dragon," because his father had been a knight of the Christian Order of the Drakul or Dragon. The Turks nicknamed him "the Impaler," because he condemned many of his enemies to this gruesome death but there is no record that he ever drank blood. Although he was probably not particularly evil or cruel when compared to other rulers of his day, Vlad was one of the first men to get a "bad press," because his enemies circulated stories about his atrocities in the first pamphlets ever printed in Europe. In his native Romania, however, Vlad is remembered as a just ruler who defended his country from the Turks. He died in battle in 1576, and was buried at the Snagov Monastery. His body has never been found.

Traditional wooden architecture has been preserved in the historic cities and villages of the Carpathians.

WHEN TO VISIT

The mountainous Transylvanian region has a marked continental climate, with very cold winters—plenty of snow for winter sports—and hot summers, suitable for high-altitude hiking. The snow can stay on the ground as late as May, so the hiking season begins in late spring-early summer. To avoid the worst of the heat and cold, visit in May-June and September-October. Folk traditions are very much alive in Transylvania, and fairs and festivals take place throughout the year; the Fundata Fair near Bran originated as a marriage market; July and August feature cultural and music festivals in Bran and Sighisoara; and Bran also holds a traditional Christmas fair.

Giants of the Deep

WHALE-WATCHING IN ICELAND

An island of marine wonders tucked away on the edge of the frozen northern ocean, Iceland is a place of many contrasts. Close enough to the Arctic Circle for its seas to freeze over in winter, it is warmed by the constantly erupting fires of the earth.

Appearing from the depths without warning, these giants of the ocean will astound you both by their size and their gentleness.

WHALES OF ICELAND

Icelandic waters are home to both toothed whales, which eat fish, and baleen whales, which sift krill and plankton from the water. The main species of toothed whales are brown-colored northern bottlenose whales (20–30 feet, 7–10 m); sperm whales (50–60 feet, 17–20 m), whose most prominent feature is their enormous heads; long-finned pilot whales, which are most commonly seen in late summer and fall; the white and black orcas, the famous killer whales, which are easily identified by their tall dorsal fin; and harbor porpoises (4.5–6 feet, 1.5–2 m), which often swim in huge pods up to 250 strong.

The baleen whales include humpbacks, (33–55 feet, 11–19 m); the smallest and most common baleen whales, minkes (24–30 feet, 8–10 m); fin whales (54–80 feet, 18–27 m), which have a distinctive gray and white coloration; sei whales (35–60 feet, 12–20 m), which are very dark in color and whose spouts are 9 feet (3 m) high; and the giants of the deep, blue whales, which are the largest animal ever to live on Earth. The largest blue whale ever recorded was over 100 feet (33 m) long and weighed some 200 tons. They can be spotted far off from their spouts that reach 18–27 feet (6–9 m) high.

"Alone in Iceland you are alone indeed, and the homeless, undisturbed wilderness gives something of its awful calm to the spirit." Miss Oswald, 1882

WHERE

Since the age of its first Vikings settlers, Iceland has been home to dauntless seafarers and skilled fishermen. Its chill waters have some of the world's richest fishing grounds, and some of its greatest concentrations of seabirds and sea mammals. Once threatened by extinction, the whales of Iceland are now providing a livelihood for their erstwhile hunters, who have become the strongest advocates of their conservation. Wherever you travel around the Icelandic coast, you will have the opportunity to set out on the open sea in pursuit of these mighty lords of the ocean. But Iceland has still more to offer the visitor. With a population of less than 300,000, the island provides unique areas of unspoiled wilderness, which are literally "out of this world." You would have to travel very far—perhaps as far as Mars or Titan—to find stranger landscapes than those you will encounter here: Active volcanoes spew molten rock across vast lava fields; sulfurous mud pools bubble like giant cauldrons; and geysers send plumes of water and steam hundreds of feet into the air.

WHAT TO DO

* The waters all around Iceland are so rich in whales both large and small that whale-watching cruises depart from most of the island's ports during the tourist season (April to October). Catamaran cruises operate from Reykjavik daily. But for the ruggedness of its mountain scenery, go to Husavik in northeast Iceland where you will be able to follow the whales in traditional wooden sailing sloops. Western Iceland offers cruising in bays and fjords where you can observe huge colonies of sea birds, as well as large populations of whales and dolphins.

* After a day at sea, what could be better than to relax in the warm waters of a hot spring? The most famous, the man-made Blue Lagoon, a forty-minute drive from Reykjavik, has waters of a vivid milky-blue color. The mineral-rich white mud and blue water, which are heated to 104°F (40°C), are said to have many health-giving and curative qualities.

* The English word "geyser" comes from Geysir, the name of Iceland's most famous blowhole in southwest Iceland, which propels a column of scalding water up to 260 feet (80 m) into the air. Unfortunately Geysir is not as dependable as it once was, but the nearby Strokkur (the Churn) blows up to 115 feet (35 m) every five to ten minutes.

* The best time to see Gullfloss, the 105-foot (32 m) "Golden Falls," is on a fine spring or summer's day, when the swirling clouds of mist surrounding the falls are filled with shimmering rainbows.

* Lake Myvatn, in the northeast of the island, and its surrounding area is one of the world's strangest natural wonders. Around the cobalt-blue lake, which teems with water birds, you will be able to see boiling mud pits, and lava fields and deserts dominated by huge contorted lava pillars. After your exertions, you can bathe in the naturally heated thermal waters of the Viti volcanic crater.

* On a clear day in Reykjavik, you can gaze northwest and catch sight of the shining Snaefellsjokull glacier, 60 miles (96 km) away on the Snaefellsnes Peninsula. Although not the largest of Iceland's many glaciers, it is one of the most accessible and popular with both locals and visitors.

* Helgafell, the sacred mountain that figures prominently in Icelandic sagas where the first Icelandic parliament met in the ninth century, is in reality little more than a large hill at 240 feet (73 m). The mountain still retains its ancient magic, however, and legend has it that those who climb it are entitled to three wishes.

* Jokulsargljufur ("glacial river canyon") National Park is known as "Iceland's Grand Canyon" because it boasts the island's deepest river gorge. Other sights include unusual rock formations, volcanic caves, and many waterfalls.

Wash the cares of the day away in the steaming, brightly colored waters of the Blue Lagoon.

WHEN TO VISIT

Although the island does not live up to its name as the land of ice, even in the depths of winter, the best time to visit is in summer, when you will get the best of the weather (average temperatures hover around the 50s°F (the teens in centigrade), and be able to witness the island's many maritime festivals. The tourist season ends in early fall when most attractions close down until the following spring.

Crowded though the world is, there are still many surprises awaiting the intrepid traveler.

OFF-TRACK ADVENTURE

Take a step into the unknown
and discover the unexpected on these
off-the-beaten-track adventure
vacations: The wilderness of
New Zealand's South Island will
captivate you with the variety and
drama of its landscapes; along jungle
tracks that humans abandoned more
than 1,000 years ago, explore the
ghost cities of the Maya; if as a child
you thrilled to the stories told by
Jack London, journey to his world
in the northern remote corner of
Alaska; or seek out the exotic and
exciting in the tropical kingdoms of
Southeast Asia.

A Journey to Middle Earth

New Zealand's South Island

With landscapes so impressive and varied that it was chosen to play the part of G.R.R. Tolkein's Middle Earth in "The Lord of the Rings" trilogy, South Island has everything from dramatic mountain peaks and glaciers, to fjords and sandy beaches, ancient rain forests, lakes, and open grasslands.

At times tranquil and relaxing, at others awe-inspiring and invigorating, the landscapes of New Zealand's South Island will never fail to impress and entertain the vacationer.

"It was junior England all the way to Christchurch—in fact, just a garden." Mark Twain, 1873

WHERE

The islands of New Zealand were among the last places on earth to be settled by humans. The Polynesian Maori arrived in their ocean-going canoes about 1,000 years ago. They settled mainly in the warmer North Island, leaving large tracts of the South Island as virgin wilderness. Even today, the majority of New Zealand's population lives in the north. The city of Christchurch, halfway down the east coast of South Island, is your natural base of operations for a visit, as it has an international airport, plenty of accommodations, and car and camper van rental agents. It is a charming and very British-looking city of detached bungalows fronted by neat gardens and a town square with an Anglican cathedral in the high Victorian style. A good plan to visit the island is to cross the central mountain ridge to the west coast, travel south toward the tip of the island, and head back along the east coast, zigzagging into the interior to take in the attractions on your way to and from Christchurch.

LOCAL KNOWLEDGE

South Island is an off-track adventurer's dream. There is a wide range of terrains to explore and they are accessible by every imaginable means of transport: hiking, cycling, camping van, and driving, as well as by an extremely good public transit system, which is inexpensive and safe. Renting a camper is a good way to travel, and you will find well-equipped camping grounds everywhere, which provide berths for vans and cabins for car drivers without their own campers or tents. And if a local asks you if you'd enjoy "a good tramp," he or she is not making some kind of risqué suggestion about you spending time with a shady lady, but asking whether you'd enjoy going for a hike.

WHEN TO VISIT

In contrast to the subtropical North Island, South Island has a mild, temperate climate, with four well-defined seasons; the weather can be unpredictable, so always pack rainwear. Winter will see snow in the far south, the highlands, and southern Alps, making it good winter-sports territory, and summer in Christchurch is warm enough to take advantage of the area's beaches. The warm and cold months are reversed, as this is the Southern Hemisphere, and the busiest time is over the school summer vacation from late December to late January. However, even during peak periods, you will find plenty of unpopulated wilderness on South Island, which is an ideal place to get away from it all, but if you are heading for the busier attractions over the holiday season, best to book ahead.

WHAT TO DO

* When walking through Christchurch's leafy center along the banks of the River Avon, the visitor might be forgiven for thinking that he or she had somehow been transported to rural England—everything is green and cultivated, the scale is human, and the pace of life, relaxed. But appearances can be deceptive, and the country around the city has some wild, dramatic hiking trails with bracing ocean views, as well as sandy beaches and secluded coves for swimming and sunbathing.

* New Zealand is on the Pacific "Ring of Fire" and has many hot spring resorts, the most famous of which is Rotorua on North Island. Much more tranquil are the Hanmer Springs (93 miles/150 km) and Maruia Springs (125 miles/200 km) west of Christchurch. Maruia is an ideal place to get away from it all, as it has no TVs, no landline phones, and no cell phone reception.

Rudyard Kipling described Milford Sound as the "Eighth Wonder of the World."

breathtaking views without the effort, there are helicopter and small aircraft flights that sweep over the peaks and glaciers.

* The Lake Wanaka area is a year-round playground. In summer, you can hike the trails around the lake, swim, or go boating on the clear blue waters. In winter, the Cardrona and the Treble Cone ski slopes beckon.

* If you are overdosing on nature and need a taste of urban living, drop into Queenstown on Lake Wakatipu. This compact little town has stylish hotels, bars, and restaurants, and designer shopping. But here too, nature is never far, with trails into the hills, and cruises on the lake. Daily flights link Queenstown to the main cities of New Zealand and Australia.

* The climax of any visit to South Island is Fjordland, a landscape of extraordinary drama with waterfalls, deep fjords, and towering peaks, which always delights and awes the visitor. Among the watery wonders are Milford and Doubtful sounds, the haunts of seals, dolphins, and penguins, which you can explore by kayak or cruise ship. The area features several of the world's most spectacular hiking trails: the Routeburn (in Mt. Aspiring National Park), the Hollyford, the Kepler, and the Milford tracks.

The majesty of the cloud-piercing Aoraki Mount Cook can be appreciated both from the ground and from the air.

* Even at the height of summer, you can emerge from the rain forest and suddenly find yourself confronted by a giant wall of ice. The Franz Joseph and Fox glaciers on the west coast are accessible year-round on guided ice treks.

* The very adventurous and hardy can challenge New Zealand's highest peak, Aoraki Mount Cook (12,316 feet/3,754 m) on a guided climb via the Linda Glacier, which takes between 15 and 18 hours. For those who want the

Lost Cities of the Jungle

MAYAN TRAIL OF THE PETEN

Imagine walking along a jungle track—you stumble across a stone stairway richly carved with strange hieroglyphic inscriptions partially hidden by the dense undergrowth. Such was the experience of the nineteenth- and twentieth-century rediscoverers of the lost Mayan cities of the Peten.

Many Mayan cities, like Palenque, shown here, have been restored and reconstructed piece by piece like giant puzzles.

THE RIDDLE OF THE MAYA

The great Classic Mayan sites of the Peten were occupied from the early centuries B.C. until they were abandoned in the ninth century. Despite their phenomenal achievements in the fields of mathematics, architecture, painting, and sculpture, the Maya were a technologically primitive people, who lacked the wheel, the plow, and draft animals, meaning that there was a limit both to their agricultural production and the amount of food they could import into their cities. One theory holds that the Maya were so successful in the first centuries of our era that their populations grew into the millions. However, the slash-and-burn agriculture that sustained them could not produce enough food to keep pace with their needs. Deforestation compounded by drought led to famine, epidemics, war, and civil disorder, which caused the final collapse of Classic Maya civilization.

"Nothing ever impressed me more forcibly than the spectacle of this once great and lovely city, overturned, desolate, and lost; discovered by accident, overgrown with trees for miles around, and without a name to distinguish it."
J.L. Stephens on Palenque, 1841

WHERE

The Yucatan peninsula forms the hump to the north of the Central American isthmus, covering parts of southern Mexico, Guatemala, and the former British colony of Belize. From a millennia or so B.C.E. to the coming of the Spanish conquistadors in the sixteenth century, the area was home to one of the most extraordinary civilizations of the Americas, the Maya. The very name conjures images of mysterious cities lost in dense tropical forests, steep-sided pyramids where dark gods were worshipped and from which astronomer-priests charted the course of the planets and stars, sculptures of astounding complexity and beauty, and at the heart of it all, an enigma: Why did the Maya abandon their great cities? The Maya world is divided into three contrasting zones: the southern highlands, the dense central jungles of the Peten, and the more arid north of Yucatan. Each was home to different flowerings of Mayan civilization. This trip concentrates on the classic Maya world (250–900 C.E.), centered on the cities of Tikal, Palenque, Copan, Calakmul, and dozens of other sites that are still emerging from the jungle. The main Mayan cities are easily accessible by air or road, but the more intrepid can opt to trek along jungle tracks to visit the most recently discovered sites.

WHAT TO DO

* Flores, the capital of the region and gateway to its many Mayan sites, though now an unremarkable if charming Guatemalan town, has an unusual history. Hidden deep in the impenetrable jungles of the Peten, it was the last surviving pagan Mayan kingdom, resisting Christianity and Spanish rule until the seventeenth century.

* The most accessible Mayan site in the Peten is Tikal, not far from the city of Flores. It has an airstrip and good facilities for visitors. Although this means that Tikal can be quite crowded, it is also the most extensively explored and best-restored city in the region. The central palace complexes and pyramids have been cleared of the encroaching vegetation, but the site is so extensive that there are jungle-choked ruins aplenty for those explorers who cannot make it to the more isolated sites. Highlights include seeing the sunrise from Temple IV, a building featured in the movie *Star Wars*.

* One of the most important classic Mayan sites, Calakmul was the center of a Maya "empire," which controlled a number of neighboring towns, including Caracol, Dos Pilas, and Naranjo. It is set in the middle of the Calakmul Rainforest Biosphere Natural Reserve, in the Mexican state of Campeche, 19 miles (30 km) from the Guatemalan border.

* One of the best-preserved Mexican Mayan sites is Palenque in Mexican Chiapas, famous for its multistory palace watchtower, its Temple of the Cross, and the discovery deep within one of its pyramids of one of the richest royal burials in Central America.

Today, Yucatan is still home to the Mayan people.

✶ Belize, formerly British Honduras, has more in common with the Caribbean than with its Central American neighbors. It has two Mayan sites of note: the late preclassic site of Lamanai, which was occupied until the Spanish conquest, and the classic period site Xunantunich, which was abandoned in the tenth century.

✶ Well worth a daytrip into Honduras just across its border with Guatemala is the site of Copan. Rediscovered in the nineteenth century, Copan is the site that led to the revival of interest in all things Mayan. The town, set amid rolling verdant countryside rather than jungle, is particularly rich in well-preserved inscriptions and relief sculptures.

Many Mayan cities were so large that only the densely built centers, with their temples and pyramids, have so far been excavated.

WHEN TO VISIT

The best time to visit the area is during the dry season from November to May. Naturally, this coincides with the northern winter and Christmas holidays, so many of the attractions will be busy, especially in the more developed north of Yucatan around the resort of Cancun. July through November sees rains and hurricanes, and the unpaved roads to some of the more isolated Peten sites become impassable. Rainy season also means an increased risk of malaria, but as the malaria mosquito is endemic in the region, you should take antimalarial prophylaxis (see introduction, p.9–10) whenever you are visiting. A good time to visit Guatemala is during the high feasts and holidays of the Catholic Church, such as Easter and Ascension, when you will be able to witness the mixture of Catholic worship and pagan tradition that characterizes the religious practices of the Mayan world. If you wish to combine visits to Mayan sites and a beach holiday, head for the northern coast of Yucatan, near the site of Chichen-Itza, or base yourself in Belize.

The Call of the Wild

THE ALASKAN WILDERNESS

If you are old, go there. But if you are young, wait. The scenery of Alaska is much grander than anything else in the world and it is not good to dull one's capacity for enjoyment by seeing the finest first.

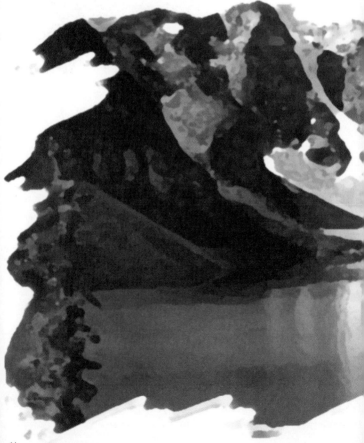

WHERE

Anchorage is big-city Alaska, home to more than a quarter million people—nearly half the state's population. That makes Anchorage an anomaly in a state where the featured attraction is the wilderness. Alaska's residents joke that visitors can't really claim to have seen the state until they leave Anchorage. The city has shopping malls, national discount stores, movie theaters, fast-food restaurants, high-rise hotels, and a busy international airport. But, as with most places in Alaska, the wilderness is never far away. The snowy Chugach Mountains rise just behind the city, and some of the state's premier natural attractions are within a day's travel: Denali National Park, the Kenai Peninsula, Katmai National Park, and Portage Glacier. These sights—and Anchorage's status as the state's primary transportation hub—are the reasons that nearly all travelers to Alaska make this their first port of call.

Even in the United States, where visitors will encounter many natural and human superlatives, the vastness and beauty of the Alaskan wilderness will leave them astounded and exhilarated.

"To the lover of wilderness, Alaska is one of the most wonderful countries in the world." John Muir, Founder of *The Sierra Club*

WHAT TO DO

* Alaska is an adventurer's dream. Sweeping scenic views, vast wilderness lands, glaciers, and wildlife offer the visitor an experience unparalleled anywhere. From dense forests rich in wildlife, to the snow-capped peaks and majestic glaciers, Alaska is a true wilderness adventure.

* From Anchorage, venture to the Kenai Peninsula. Outdoor activities abound in Seward, gateway to Kenai Fjords National Park. Hike in the high country of the Harding icefields, or enjoy a spectacular cruise through Resurrection Bay and Aialik Fjord with views of local marine life, migrating birds, and tidewater glaciers along this remote wilderness coast. Perhaps even try your hand fishing the ice-blue waters.

* After leaving the Kenai Peninsula, you can ride the Alaska Marine Highway ferry through Prince William Sound to Valdez. Sit back and relax as you glide past the rugged coastline along the snow-capped Chugach Mountains that rise from the sea here, past icebergs released by the immense Columbia Glacier, and the myriad of forested islands that dot our way to Valdez.

* The towering mountains that surround this fjord offer stunning views and what better way to experience this beauty than with a sea-kayaking trip? A variety of hiking trails also make this area a walker's paradise.

* The Alaska pipeline that spans over 800 miles (1,280 km) to the coast of the Arctic Ocean offers guided tours of its southern terminus here as well.

* After this, you can follow the most beautiful drive in Alaska, climbing Thompson Pass and past Wrangell Saint Elias National Park. As you travel the old Denali Highway, keep an eye open for caribou and other wildlife while enjoying the peaceful, unspoiled wilderness en route to the Denali National Park. Surrounding Mt. McKinley, the tallest peak in North America, Denali offers a vast refuge for a variety of wildlife. Wolves, caribou, and Dall sheep call Denali home, as well as the mighty grizzly bear.

* Scenic bus tours are available to take you through the pristine backcountry of the park, offering excellent opportunities to see these majestic animals in their natural habitat and the incredible views this unique landscape of tundra and taiga presents. A range of optional activities is available, including river rafting, scenic flights, dogsled demonstrations, and hiking options for all fitness and adventure levels.

WHEN TO VISIT

Anchorage has a cold maritime climate, with cool summers and frosty winters. The average annual temperature is a chilly 36°F (2°C). The area gets only around 15 in (40 cm) of rain annually, but expect cloudy weather—more than 50 percent of the time—in summer. The city receives an average of 69 in (175 cm) of snow annually, nearly all of it falling October–April. June–August high temperatures are commonly in the 60s°F (high teens °C) and can reach into the upper 70s°F (mid-20s°C) on warm days. Winter temperatures are cold (but much milder than in interior Alaska), with typical January nights around 6°F (-14°C). Anchorage never gets completely dark in the middle of summer, and the midsummer's day is a time for celebration, with nearly 19.5 hours of daylight.

Of course, the reverse is true in winter, and by the winter solstice in late December, the city sees only about five hours of daylight.

AURORA BOREALIS: THE NORTHERN LIGHTS

Because of the long days and mild conditions, summer is when the vast majority of travelers go to Alaska. But winter also attracts its share of visitors, including hardy souls who come to take in the spectacular Northern Lights or to enjoy a dog sledding adventure. The Northern Lights are best viewed between Fairbanks and Barrow. Mayo and Faro, Yukon, north of Whitehorse, is also ideally situated for great viewing.

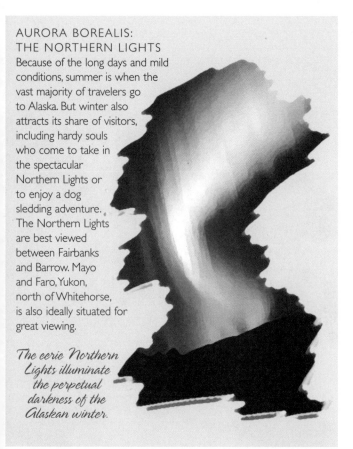

The eerie Northern Lights illuminate the perpetual darkness of the Alaskan winter.

Kingdoms of the South

SOUTHEAST ASIA

Discover the unspoiled charms of Southeast Asia. From deserted tropical beaches and remote rain forest trails, to archeological wonders, sleepy colonial cities, and bustling metropolises, you will find something to enthrall and fascinate you in these ancient Asian kingdoms that are awakening from the sleep of centuries.

WHERE

The countries of Laos, Vietnam, and Cambodia once made up the French colonial territory of Indochina, which gives them a distinct Gallic flavor. This region, which has seen so much sorrow and strife since the end of World War II, is fast developing into one of the world's most exciting tourist destinations. Hurry, before everyone else gets there first! Laos remains the most isolated and least-known of the three countries. Here you will be able to discover Southeast Asian life as it has been lived for thousands of years. The biggest draw in Cambodia is the Khmer temple complexes of Angkor, but visitors should not overlook the charms of its countryside and French colonial capital. A booming postwar economy, stunning scenery, an unspoiled coastline, and a rich historical and cultural heritage combine to make Vietnam the up-and-coming destination in Southeast Asia, meaning that, one day, it will equal or even surpass Thailand's position as leader of the region's tourism.

LOCAL KNOWLEDGE

Visitors to the area should make sure that their vaccinations are up to date (see introduction, p.9). Water- and food-borne diseases such as cholera, typhoid, and hepatitis are prevalent, and you should take precautions with food and drink. The most sensible is to drink bottled water (watch the ice), and avoid eating seafood and uncooked foods in establishments that might not look as if they maintain the best hygiene standards. Diseases spread by insects are also common, including malaria and dengue fever, two infections spread by mosquitoes. While malaria can be warded off with prophylaxis (see introduction, p.9–10), no such treatment exists against dengue fever, which may have potentially fatal complications. Preventing bites both day and night is the best policy. You should cover as much skin as is comfortable, wear insect repellent, and sleep under a mosquito net at night.

The cities of the former colony of French Indochina combine the joys of Asian exoticism with Gallic charm.

WHAT TO DO

✴ The capital of Laos is the former French colonial town of Vientiane on the Mekong River. Like its immediate neighbors, Laos is a Buddhist country, and the ornate Wat Si Saket is the most venerable shrine in the capital.

✴ Another Lao city famous for its many Buddhist foundations is the small town of Luang Prabang 130 miles (209 km) northwest of the capital; combine with a visit to the nearby Buddhist Pak Ou caves.

✴ Another former French colonial city, Phnom Penh also boasts many ancient Buddhist landmarks. Among the leading attractions are the Khmer Silver Pagoda and the National Museum, which fortunately survived the destructive excesses of the Khmer Rouge.

✴ Cambodia's and, undoubtedly, the region's leading attraction is Angkor located 150 miles (241 km) north of Phnom Penh. Built by the Khmer between the ninth and thirteenth centuries, the more than 100 sacred precincts were abandoned to the jungle in 1431. The three largest and most impressive temples are Angkor Thom, Ta Prohm, and Angkor Wat.

✴ The Vietnamese capital of Hanoi is fast being transformed from a sleepy postcolonial city to an economic powerhouse with skyscrapers that rival anything in Hong Kong or Shanghai. The Hanoi of days gone by survives in the Old and French quarters.

✴ The charming highland town of Dalat was selected by the Emperor Bao as the site of his summer

Abandoned by its creators in 1481, the vast temple complex at Angkor forms Cambodia's main cultural attraction.

palace, and by the French as the place to get away from the lowland heat and humidity. Long popular with Vietnamese honeymooners, this "City of Love" has a laid-back, café-culture atmosphere.

∗ Featured in many ad campaigns and movies, the enchanted Halong Bay contains some 3,000 eccentrically shaped islets. On a romantic junk cruise or paddling your own kayak, you will be able to discover the bay's deserted island beaches and the huge caves carved out by the waves.

∗ The city of Hue is one of the cultural highlights of Vietnam. A former imperial capital, the city has many palaces and temples, as well as the imperial tombs of the Nguyen dynasty.

∗ If you need a break from the hectic cultural itinerary for some beachside R&R, head for the resort of Nha Trang. Its clear waters are ideal for snorkeling and scuba diving.

∗ Hoi An was one of the first ports to cater to Dutch, Portuguese, Chinese, and Japanese merchants visiting Vietnam in the sixteenth century. Over 800 historic buildings, including pagodas, temples, and private houses, have survived, creating an as yet unspoiled window onto Vietnam's history.

∗ A hill station built by the French in the 1920s on Vietnam's border with China, Sapa offers some good hiking country, a handicraft market for the area's native hill tribes, and a chance to escape the heat of the lowlands.

WHEN TO VISIT

Southeast Asia sits in the tropical and subtropical climate belt, and the weather is generally warm to very warm and humid. The greater part of the region has only two seasons, wet and dry, though their dates vary. In Cambodia, the wet season lasts from May to October, and the more isolated parts of the country may be difficult to access during the wettest months. The coolest and driest months are December and January. Rainy season in Laos is from July to October, and the peak of the tourist season is from December through February. Vietnam has the most varied

climate of the three countries. In the south, the rainy season lasts from May to November. The colder north has cool, wet winters (November through April) and hot summers (May through October).

Wat Xieng Thong is one of Luang Prabang's many Buddhist shrines.

Since classical antiquity, the continent of Europe has been one of the world's great culturals centers.

CITIES OF CULTURE

The world is full of wonders,
some natural, others man-made.
These cultural excursions will help
you discover some of the artistic
treasures of the Old World.
In "Ye Olde London Towne,"
now not so old, but youthful and
vibrant, take your seats for the latest
smash hit musical or the best in
classical tragedy; on the island of king
Minos, so legend has it, a monster
dwelt in the heart of a labyrinth—see
the truth behind the legend in
Cretan Knossos; or roll back the years
to the glories of imperial Vienna,
capital of dance and music.

The World's Stage

LONDON'S THEATERLAND

From the Elizabethan oak beams of Shakespeare's reconstructed Globe Theatre to the concrete postmodernism of the Royal National Theatre, London offers the greatest variety of theatrical entertainment anywhere on earth. Fans of the dramatic arts can enjoy a Lloyd-Webber musical, a classical tragedy, and an avant-garde play, all within a short taxi ride from their West End hotel.

WHERE

The capital of the United Kingdom needs little introduction. But for the first-time visitor, this vast metropolis of six million people can be daunting. First there is its sheer size, and then the confused jumble of its streets, which lack the order of planned cities such as New York and Washington D.C. If the aim of your trip is to sample the cultural heart of the capital, then you should stay within Zone One of the transit system, preferably in or near the commercial and entertainments district known as the "West End"

to differentiate it from the working-class "East End" and the business district, "the City," both located on the eastern side of the capital. A West End hotel does not have to be expensive, though the Ritz, Savoy, and Dorchester will cater to those with luxury tastes. Smaller, less expensive hotels can be found in Bloomsbury and Fitzrovia, which are still within walking distance of most of the capital's cultural attractions. Theatrical entertainment, however, is not limited to the West End, but can be found all over the city.

London is rightly famed for the quality of its theaters, but it should also be praised for its audiences: always enthusiatic, appreciative, and polite, without losing their critical sense.

LOCAL KNOWLEDGE

There is so much happening on the London theater scene that the visitor may have trouble finding out what is going on. Two good sources of information are *Time Out* and *What's On in London* magazines (for Web addresses, see Reference Section, p.142). Many shows, though not the ones that sell out, make tickets available for that day's performance at the Half Price Ticket Booth in Leicester Square. If tickets for a show are not available there, at your hotel, or through a ticket agency, you could try to get in line for returns at the theater itself; come to the theater a few hours before the performance you want to attend. However tempting it might seem, never buy a ticket from a "ticket tout" or scalper. Not only are their tickets overpriced, they may be forgeries, or be for restricted-view seats, which may well ruin your enjoyment of the show. If you plan to eat before your night out, many restaurants in the West End offer a "pre-theater menu," ranging in price from as little £10-£20 ($16-$32) for a meal that might normally cost you twice as much at any other time.

"More than any other city in Europe, London is a show, living by bluff and display. People have always remarked on its theatrical nature."
Jan Morris, 1980

WHAT TO DO

* The West End, London's Broadway, boasts over 30 traditional theaters providing the full range of dramatic entertainment, from hit musicals, classic drama, bedroom farces, and cutting-edge avant-garde productions. In addition, the area also contains London's top museums, a huge range of bars and restaurants, and the shopper's paradises that are Oxford and Bond streets.

* A showcase of the arts, the South Bank Centre consists of the Royal Festival Hall, the Hayward Gallery, the National Film Theatre, and the Royal National Theatre (NT). Built to be the showcase for the best in British drama, the NT contains three main stages—the Olivier, Lyttleton, and Cotteslow.

The building, which overlooks the Thames, also has exhibition areas, terraces, bars, and restaurants.

* The West End represents only one part of the London theater scene. Dozens of smaller venues, such as the Almeida in Islington, the Mermaid in Blackfriars, and the Tricycle in Kilburn, offer a huge variety of works, some of which will transfer to the West End. Check out the press listings for the latest offerings on this dynamic, fast-moving independent scene.

* On a warm summer's evening, make the pleasant walk eastward along the river from the National Theatre to the Globe Theatre, a faithful reproduction of Shakespeare's original 1599 playhouse, founded by the

The Thames provides a scenic backdrop for many of London's famous theatrical institutions.

American director and actor Sam Wanamaker. The Globe's season runs from May through September, featuring the masterworks of Shakespeare just as his contemporaries would have seen them. Linger in the riverside cafés, pubs, and restaurants that offer a range of food and drink options, either before or after the performance.

* One out-of-town theater excursion that you can make as a day trip or a one-night stopover is a visit to Shakespeare's birthplace of Stratford-upon-Avon, 83 miles (133 km) northwest of London. Stratford is one of the homes of the Royal Shakespeare Company (RSC), with three theaters offering classical and modern repertoires in addition to the performances of the Bard of Avon's major works.

A faithful reproduction of Shakespeare's original playhouse of 1599, The Globe Theatre presents the Bard's masterworks as intended by Shakespeare himself.

WHEN TO VISIT

London may have a reputation for fog, but these days, it is undeserved. The famous London "smogs," actually caused by air pollution, are a distant memory. The country's reputation for rain, however, is more than well deserved. Rainwear and umbrellas are advisable at any time of year, as is a selection of warm-weather gear, as even in summer, the temperatures can plummet to the low 50s°F (teens °C). But if you are lucky, you can sample some glorious weather between May and September during which London's parks and café culture really come into their own. London's attractions are at their busiest from July through September, when tourists flock in from the world over, but whenever you chose to visit, this 24-hour metropolis will always bustle with locals and visitors.

Island of the Bull

CRETE

Until the year 1878, no one believed that there could be any truth to the ancient Greek legend of the bull-headed monster that lived in the middle of a great labyrinth, but that year, the ruins of a 5-acre (2 ha) palace were discovered on the Mediterranean island of Crete. The palace of Knossos was the first of many Minoan sites to be unearthed on Crete and the island of Santorini.

WHERE

As the writer Saki suggested, the Mediterranean island of Crete seems to have much more history than its modest size would warrant. Conquered and occupied in turn by the Persians, Romans, Byzantines, Arabs, Venetians, and Turks, the island is now part of Greece. Remains of each of these great occupying cultures can be found on the island, which also offers dramatic natural landscapes with mountains, gorges, and towering cliffs plunging into the blue-on-blue sea. Now popular as a summer destination with northern Europeans, the island has many resorts for the vacationer, some crowded (if not to say overdeveloped) and others more tranquil, suiting the different tastes and requirements of visitors. But it is to the distant Cretan past that this journey takes you.

The great Minoan palaces were multipurpose buildings with residential quarters, temples, and public storerooms.

"The people of Crete unfortunately make more history than they can consume locally."
Saki (H.H. Munro), 1911

Minoan civilization was among the first to flourish in the Mediterranean. In the second millennium before our era, a sophisticated urban culture reigned on Crete and its neighboring islands. Until the nineteenth century, all that was known of it were the legends told by the Ancient Greeks of a blessed island ruled by the mighty King Minos.

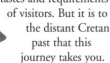

The Minoans were the first traders of the Mediterranean. From their island home of Crete, they traveled and traded far and wide.

WHAT TO DO

* A few miles southeast of the island's modern capital of Heraklion stands the Great Palace of Knossos, the legendary labyrinth of King Minos and his accursed son, the bull-headed Minotaur. The palace, which dates to 1700 B.C.E., was excavated and partially reconstructed by Sir Arthur Evans between 1900 and 1935. The vast multistoried building, which contains 1,400 rooms, was a residential complex, an administrative, ceremonial and religious center, as well as a public storehouse—imagine combining city hall, a church, a mall, and a luxury condo and you begin to get the idea. The west side of the palace contains a throne room and other ceremonial spaces, while the east side was a more intimate residential area, with apartments said to belong to the king and queen. Many of the rooms are decorated with colorful frescoes of Minoan life. Other buildings on the site include the Little Palace, the Royal Villa, the High Priest's House, the public bath, and the Royal Mortuary Temple.

* The many artworks found at Knossos and the other Minoan palaces of the island are on display in the Archaeological Museum of Heraklion, one of the finest museums in Greece.

* Believed to be the oldest Minoan palace on the island, Phaistos stands on the Mesara Plain in central Crete. Dominated by Crete's highest mountain, Mt. Ida, it has the most beautiful natural setting of any site on the island. The palace has yielded thousands of inscriptions in the mysterious Linear A script, which still defies our best attempts to decipher it.

The palace at Knossos has been restored so that visitors can wander around rooms and across courtyards where Minoan courtiers thronged some 3,700 years ago.

✴ Crete's third-largest Minoan site, Malia, is on the coast, east of Heraklion. Malia follows a similar floor plan to Knossos, but here you will be able to appreciate a Minoan palace without the crowds that throng the better-known site.

✴ The smallest of the Minoan palace, Zarkos, is on the east coast of Crete. The 150-room complex, which is the latest to have been excavated on the islands, was not looted when it was abandoned after the earthquake that destroyed it, leaving many artifacts to be discovered where they had been dropped some 3,000 years ago. The remoteness of the coastal site itself is worth a mention, and the best way to access the palace is through a narrow gorge.

✴ The remains of another ruined Minoan city, Akrotiri, was discovered buried under a thick layer of volcanic ash and debris on the island of Santorini. The island, now a gigantic sea-filled caldera, was literally blown apart by an eruption that is believed to have brought about the decline of Minoan civilization in 1650 B.C.E. Some researchers believe that the eruption—one of the largest ever known on earth—gave rise to the Greek myth of the destruction of Atlantis.

✴ A natural wonder worth exploring on Crete is the Samaria Gorge. A 10-mile (16-km) trail takes you downhill some 3,000 feet (1,000 m), narrowing to as little as 9 feet (3 m) at the Iron Gates, to emerge at the village of Agia Roumeli. In addition to stunning views, you will be able to enjoy a fine show of spring flowers and catch a glimpse of rare local wildlife. The gorge closes from mid-October and reopens sometime in April, depending on water levels.

WHEN TO VISIT

Crete, like the other Mediterranean islands, is a favored vacation destination for northern Europeans. Great stretches of the coast, and parts of the interior have been developed as resorts and vacation villages. Unless you are a sun worshipper and wish to combine a cultural tour of the island with a beach vacation, avoid the peak summer months and the crowds. The best times to visit the island are spring through early summer (May–June) and late summer through early fall (September–October), when the weather will not be too hot, but still warm enough on a good day to take advantage of the island's stunning beaches.

Crete is also the largest of the Greek Islands, and a popular summertime destination for northern Europeans.

A Little Night Music

VIENNA AND SALZBURG, AUSTRIA

Imperial Vienna is remembered as the city that gave the world the waltz. Elegant concert halls, theaters, and opera houses still grace the streets of the city that once ruled most of central Europe. Once you have sampled the musical delights of the capital, visit Salzburg, birthplace of Wolfgang Amadeus Mozart, and home of one of the world's great music festivals.

WOLFGANG AMADEUS MOZART (1756–1791)

Mozart was born into a musical family; his father, Leopold, was musician at the Salzburg court, and the young Wolfgang showed his prodigious musical ability from an early age. He began his career at the tender age of six with piano recitals all over Europe, when he astounded audiences in Vienna, London, and Paris. Mozart composed countless symphonies, concerti, and operas, including *The Marriage of Figaro*, *The Barber of Seville*, and *The Magic Flute*, but despite his talent and popularity, he had a difficult personal and professional life. He infuriated his patron, the Prince-Archbishop of Salzburg, whose employment he finally left in 1781; and he quarreled with his father over his marriage to Constanze in 1782. He died from a fever at the age of 35, leaving his final composition, the *Requiem* unfinished.

WHERE

Vienna's extravagantly crafted palaces, churches, castles, museums, opera houses, and concert halls befit its former role as the capital of Europe's oldest and largest multinational monarchy, the Austro-Hungarian Empire. The empire, heir to the Holy Roman Empire of Charlemagne, was finally dismembered at the end of World War I (1914–1918). Fallen on hard times when shorn of its former domains, Vienna was reborn as a comfortable, elegant, old-world city of the arts and culture, with a yearly round of concerts, opera, and lavish balls, where even today men in white tie and tails partner ladies in flowing satin and silk gowns to the strains of Strauss waltzes. And if the culture begins to pall a little, why not relax in one of Vienna's many coffee houses to sample Austria's trademark confectionery, *sachertorte*—death by chocolate. The ancient Episcopal city of Salzburg in western Austria was home to Mozart for over 20 years, and now hosts one of Europe's premier cultural festivals.

The Church was a major patron of music; apart from Mozart, another famous composer in its employ was J. S. Bach.

WHAT TO DO

∗ Like Paris and London, Vienna has so much to see and sample that it takes several visits to take everything in. First-timers should visit St. Stephen's Cathedral; the Ringstrasse, part of the city's ancient fortifications turned into a magnificent nineteenth-century boulevard; the splendid Schönbrunn Castle and Hofburg Imperial Palace, both imperial Hapsburg residences; and the Kunsthistoriches Museum, one of the richest fine-art collections in the world.

∗ The Christmas and New Year holidays are a magical time to visit Vienna. The city is powdered with snow and the streets garlanded with the lights of Christmas markets. The Kaiserball (Imperial Ball) at the Hofburg Imperial Palace begins the Fasching Carnival season, and the Vienna Philharmonic Orchestra's Neujahrskonzert (New Year Concert) of Strauss waltzes at the Musikverein is a sell-out event broadcast worldwide to an audience of millions.

∗ After the Kaiserball, January and February are the months of Fasching, or Austrian Carnival, when the city holds a series of balls in some of the city's grandest venues. The highlights of the season are the Opernball (Opera Ball), held in the Vienna State Opera House since 1877, and the Philharmonic Ball, held in the Musikverein Concert Hall, where the "band" is none other than the Vienna Philharmonic Orchestra itself! Less grand but no less spectacular are the Blumenball (Flower Ball), Zuckerbäckerball (Confectioners' Ball), and the Kaffeesiederball (Coffeepot Ball).

"Baroque Vienna knows that an illusion that makes you happy is better than a reality that makes you sad." Allan Whicker, 1980

WHEN TO VISIT

Situated in the mountainous heart of Europe, Austria benefits from temperate summers, which are naturally popular with visitors to its many cultural attractions, and snowy winters, which make it a center for winter sports. The musical year starts in January with the New Year concert season, followed in January and February by the Fasching (Carnival) ball season. Spring and summer see the twin highlights of the Austrian cultural year: the Vienna International Festival (May through June) and the Salzburg International Festival (five weeks beginning the last week of July).

∗ The Wiener Festwochen (Vienna International Festival) of theater, dance, and music is held in the city every year between May and June.

∗ Nestling among the Austrian Alps, Salzburg is a picturesque medieval city of snaking alleyways, castles, monasteries, palaces, and baroque churches. The 900-year-old Hohensalzburgis Fortress is one of the best-preserved medieval strongholds in Europe.

∗ The city is home to the annual Salzburger Festspiele (Salzburg International Festival), a five-week culture fest of opera, concerts, and theater.

∗ No stay in Salzburg would be complete without a visit to the Mozart museums at the Mozart family's two residences in the city. Mozart was born at 9 Getreidegasse in 1756 and lived there until 1773. This was a modest dwelling consisting of kitchen, living room, bedroom, and study. On display are Mozart's childhood violin, his clavichord, and piano.
The second, much larger residence, also a museum, is at 8 Makart Square. It is here that Mozart composed many of his most famous works. He lived there until 1780, when he left Salzburg to seek his fortune in Vienna.

The grandeur of Vienna is a fitting stage for one of the world's great music festivals.

Travel is said to exhilarate the senses and broaden the mind,
but if you pick the right destination, it can also calm them.

SPIRITUAL RETREATS

If stress is modern man's greatest enemy, then these spiritual getaways will let you rediscover the tranquility and harmony of a slower, gentler age. Study the science of yoga amid the tropical "Backwaters" of India's Kerala; follow in the footsteps of Australia's Aboriginal people along red desert paths to sacred sites of power; uncover the mystic secrets locked in the rolling hills of the peaceful English countryside; or take the pilgrim's trail to Heaven on Japan's sacred mountain peak.

A Passage to Kerala

STUDY YOGA IN SOUTHWESTERN INDIA

Yoga has long been taught in the West as a system of physical postures, or asanas. But in reality, yoga is much, much more. It is a holistic way of being, based on physical, mental, moral, and spiritual principles. Where better to study this profound but gentle science than the idyllic beachside Indian state of Kerala?

If Eden still exists anywhere on earth it is in Kerala's tranquil "Backwaters," a network of canals that weave their way from the palm-fringed ocean through dense tropical forests.

WHERE

Increasingly popular as a tourist destination for its stunning scenery, blue skies, warm hospitality, and delicious cuisine, Kerala retains all the charm of the authentic India in a relatively uncommercialized setting. Although high season can be busy by Indian standards, Kerala is far from being a package-tour destination. There are no high-rise hotels, all-inclusive resorts, or nightclubs. The people are welcoming and unaffected; the atmosphere is calm and gentle. The ever-present palm trees provide a living for many of the locals, as well as a constant backdrop to the colors and warmth, the sights and sounds, that are truly Kerala. Trivandrum is the capital of the province; built over seven hills, it is a colorful and vibrant city with good basic amenities, traditional markets, and temples—but don't expect a shopping mall. The glory of the area is its "Backwaters," a network of waterways threaded through the beautiful tapestry of the tropical forest. Set amid this Garden of Eden are several centers offering instruction in the ancient discipline of yoga, affording the visitor the opportunity to de-stress the mind, spirit, and body.

WHAT TO DO

* A recent development in tourism, the yoga vacation is becoming an increasingly popular option for those who want to combine a conventional beach vacation with a spiritual retreat. Kerala offers a range of options: yoga resorts, drop-in centers, and traditional ashrams.

* The Beach and Lake resort is a small Ayurvedic resort (Ayurveda is the ancient system of traditional Indian medicine), located on an island 5 miles (8 km) south of Trivandrum airport. The resort offers Ayurvedic treatments, and courses in yoga and the local martial art, Kalaripayattu.

* Lighthouse Beach in Kovalam, 10 miles (16 km) from Trivandrum, offers sun worshippers breathtaking golden sands fringed with palm trees. The sea at Kovalam is great for swimming, but currents can be quite strong, so be wary. There are lifeguards during the tourist season and flagged areas for safe swimming. You can also use the swimming pools at a number of hotels for a nominal daily charge. The town has a range of accommodations and is a good base to explore the surrounding area.

* You will find the Shanti Bhavan (House of Peace) yoga center nestling on the hillside among the coconut palms in Green Valley, five minutes from Kovalam. The yoga shala on the roof, covered by dried palm leaves, provides a cool practice area surrounded by greenery. The retreat is an ideal place to deepen your understanding of yoga with a traditional Indian teacher.

* Kovalam shopping yields rich souvenirs; particularly good are the tailors who can make you an outfit or copy an existing one for a fraction of the cost of made-to-order in Europe or the United States. Bring any item of clothing you want copied, and select from the colorful local silks and printed cottons to have it made up.

* Good day trips include: Kanyakumari on the most southerly point, Ponmudi Hill Station in the Cardamom hills, Neyyar Dam with the Shivananda Yoga Ashram, and Lion Park.

* Traveling further along the coast, you can visit Alleppey and spend the night on a converted rice boat or take the all-day backwater cruise to Quilon, perhaps stopping at Vallikavu to get *darshan* (a blessing) from Amma, a renowned local guru.

* Come inland to Thekkady to visit the Periyar Wildlife Sanctuary, then travel up 5,400 feet (1,800 m) into the hills of the Southern Ghats to reach Munnar Hill Station and tea plantations. Travel by local bus and train to have a real picture of India, finding accommodations as you go.

*"One should practice the asanas, which give the yogi strength,
keep him in good health, and make his limbs supple."*

Hatha Yoga Pradipika

WHEN TO VISIT

The vacation season for southwestern India is October through April, when the weather will be hot but not too stifling or humid. June and July see the arrival of the local monsoon to the area, with heavy daily rainfalls and flooding in low-lying areas. South India has its fair share of health problems, so make sure your vaccinations are up to date and take antimosquito precautions (see p.9–10). On a trip to South India, a friendly hotel owner gave me a particularly effective local antibug preparation containing citronella extract, which had the added benefit of smelling a lot better than some of the chemical insect repellents.

LOCAL CUISINE

Sadya, the typical Kerala feast served on a banana leaf, is a sumptuous spread of rice and more than 14 vegetable dishes, topped with "*payasam*," a delicious sweet dessert cooked in milk.

As in much of South India, vegetarian food is popular. However, you also find tasty nonvegetarian dishes, such as *pathiri* and *kozhi* curry (chicken), spicy *biriyani*, and fish dishes. There are many restaurants and cafés serving local seafood; the prawn curry in coconut gravy is exceptionally good. Almost every dish prepared in Kerala has coconut and spices to flavor the local cuisine, giving it a sharp pungency that is heightened with the use of tamarind, while coconut gives it its richness, absorbing some of the tongue-teasing, pepper-hot flavors. Tender coconut water is a refreshing nutritious thirst quencher. The crunchy *papadam*, banana, and jackfruit chips can give fries a run for their money any day.

More than an exercise system of static postures, yoga teaches a holistic approach to living.

Singing the Land

THE RED CENTER OF AUSTRALIA

Uluru, formally known as Ayers Rock, is not only one of the natural icons of the continent-sized country of Australia, it is also the sacred symbol of the profoundly spiritual but still little-understood lore of its native Aboriginal peoples.

Uluru, the worlds largest freestanding rock, marks the "Red Center" of the great continent-sized country of Australia.

WHERE

The Uluru-Kata Tjuta National Park, located in the southern half of the Northern Territory, is also known as the "Red Center" of Australia, from the rich red color of it's iron-rich sands and rocks. Its most famous attraction, the awesome Uluru, is a single, massive, freestanding domed rock—in other words, a giant pebble—that extends some 3 miles (5 km) below the surface of the desert, and rises 1,122 feet (342 m) above it. Uluru, however, is only one of the many natural wonders that will awe the visitor to the area, which includes sand dunes, as well as the exotic fauna and flora of Australia. The national park is administered by the traditional owners of the land, the Anangu Aboriginal people, and Uluru and the other natural features of the park form an integral part of their beliefs, which you can discover in the area's colorful traditional paintings, sometimes called "dreamings."

TJUKURPA

The English words "Dreamtime" and "Dreaming" are often used to translate the Aboriginal word *Tjukurpa*, which is the term used for the creation stories and traditional lore of the Australian Aboriginal peoples. These translations imply that these beliefs are somehow unreal but *Tjukurpa* does not have any connotation of illusion or unreality. In the Anangu creation story, the world is unformed and empty until ancestral beings—people, plants, and animals—move across the land, creating the landscape and its fauna and flora. The spirits of these beings still dwell on the land and act as its guardians. *Tjukurpa* includes religion, law, and custom; the past, present, and future; the relationship between people, plants, animals, and the land; and the ceremonies that maintain the balance and harmony between humans and their environment. *Tjukurpa* is the subject of many of the artwork that you will be able to see and purchase in the area.

WHAT TO DO

✳ You can fly directly to Yulara's Connellan Airport from Australia's major cities or drive the 200 miles (320 km) southwest of Alice Springs to Yulara (formerly Ayer's Rock Resort), where you can find a range of accommodations just outside the Uluru-Kata Tjuta National Park, 12 miles (19 km) away.

✳ The Uluru base walk (6 miles/ 10 km) takes between two and four hours depending on your pace and whether you linger to enjoy the ever-changing views of the rock. Special viewing areas to photograph the sunrise and sunset have been set up on the trail. The base walk is an excellent alternative to climbing the rock, which, though not forbidden, is not encouraged because of the sacred nature of the site. The clockwise walk is rarely crowded and takes in the Mala and Mutitjulu trails along the way.

✳ A free guided Mala Trail is conducted daily from the base of Uluru. A ranger will guide you along a shaded track, stopping to explain Australian Aboriginal stories associated with Mala ancestors, rock art, the traditional Anangu lifestyle, their history, and environment.

✳ Another unforgettable site at either dawn or dusk is Kata Tjuta (formerly "The Olgas"), a series of 36 domed rocks 22.5 miles (36 km) west of Uluru. Although perhaps not as dramatic as the giant Uluru, Kata Tjuta has an even more mysterious atmosphere. Geologists believe that Kata Tjuta may have once been a single rock even larger than Uluru, but that has been eroded over millions of years into the separate outcrops you see today.

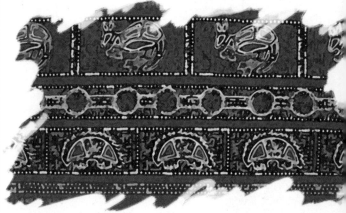

Australian aboriginal artworks are striking for their use of pattern and color, but they also convey complex stories that explain humanity's relationship to nature.

✴ After seeing The Olgas of Kata Tjuta, view its sand dunes from dune-top platforms that provide seating, shade, and visitor information.

✴ In the evening you could opt to eat under the desert sky at the Sounds of Silence Dinner. You arrive in time to see the sun setting over Uluru and Kata Tjuta, before digging into a gourmet lantern-lit meal. Between the main course and dessert, an astronomer gives a talk about the starlit sky, where you will see the Southern Cross, the Southern Hemisphere's most famous constellation, and the Milky Way, which is usually almost impossible to make out in our polluted city skies.

✴ Ride a "ship of the desert"— a camel—to see the sunrise or sunset in the desert. Camels are not native to Australia but were introduced there as pack animals in the nineteenth century. Many have since gone back to the wild, and herds of the Arabian beast can be seen side by side with kangaroos in the Outback.

✴ An enterprise owned and managed by the local Anangu people, the traditional owners of Uluru-Kata Tjuta operate the Kuniya and Liru trails. On the walk, Anangu guides teach you about *Tjukurpa* traditional lore and demonstrate their bush skills.

LOCAL KNOWLEDGE

When hiking in the Australian "Outback," safety should be your main priority. Every year, visitors from more temperate climes suffer from heatstroke and heat exhaustion—conditions that can easily be avoided by taking a few common-sense precautions: always wear a hat and plenty of sunscreen to ward off the worst of the heat and sun; carry one liter (approx. 2 pints) of water with you for each hour you plan to be walking, and always stay on the marked trail. The areas sacred to the Anangu people in the park are fenced off, so please respect their beliefs by not entering or photographing these sites.

WHEN TO VISIT

The Antipodean winter and summer are reversed from those of the Northern Hemisphere, but in the Red Center of Australia, you will encounter a classic desert climate—daytime temperatures range from 77°F (25°C) to 95°F (35°C), but nighttime temperatures can drop as low as 32°F (0°C)— so come prepared with both warm- and cold-weather gear. Wear layers that you can take off and put on as required. Rainfall is unpredictable in the desert, but when it rains, it literally pours, and the landscape is transformed as dry riverbeds fill with water, millions of birds appear out of nowhere, and the desert blooms.

The Enchanted Land

Across the peaceful English countryside, hidden lines of energy radiate from ancient centers of power, marked by standing stones, earthen barrows, and stone circles, the most famous of which is Stonehenge. Later religious foundations stand on some of these lines of power, including several of the country's most famous churches and monasteries.

WHERE

The countryside of southwest England is the very picture of nature that has been tamed and civilized. The gentle contours of the land have been molded by generations of farmers. Hedgerows enclose neatly tended fields and pasturelands; thatched cottages and ancient churches cluster around well-mown village greens, where white-clad gentlemen play cricket on summer afternoons. But this tranquility conceals another aspect of Britain's heritage: a land of sacred sites situated on prehistoric lines of power, known as "ley lines," where mysterious phenomena— "crop circles" and UFO sightings—are frequent occurrences. Counties like Wiltshire and Somerset, just

Glastonbury Tor dominates the surrounding countryside.

a few hours drive from London, are the hotspots of this "other" England. The great monuments of Stonehenge and Avebury stand as witnesses to the skills and arcane knowledge of distant ancestors; the great Christian centers of Salisbury and Glastonbury are the products of later ages, but harbor just as many mysteries.

Glastonbury Abbey is linked to numerous legends. Some believe that it once sheltered the Holy Grail; others that it was the burial place of King Arthur and Queen Guinevere.

THE MYSTERY OF "CROP CIRCLES"

Every summer in July and August before harvest time, mysterious patterns appear in the fields of southwest England, especially around Avebury, Glastonbury, and Salisbury. To some these "crop circles" are hoaxes carried out by human "circle makers," to others they are messages from higher intelligences, either from another plane of existence or from other worlds, as some claim to have seen UFOs just before the circles appear. Whatever you choose to believe, many of the patterns created are of great complexity and beauty, sometimes incorporating hundreds of elements over an area of many hundreds of square feet.

WHAT TO DO

✳ Salisbury, 81 miles (129 km) southwest of London, is your base of operations for an investigation of the mystery-rich counties of Wiltshire and Somerset. The historic city of Salisbury has one of England's finest Gothic cathedrals, built in the thirteenth century, as the jewel among its many fine medieval buildings.

✳ Between the years 3500 B.C.E. and 1500 B.C.E., the Celtic peoples of western Europe built some 1,000 stones circles, and more than 80 henges (circular structures made of wood or stone, which were used as astronomical observatories and temples). The most famous henge is, of course, Stonehenge, which is located on Salisbury Plain, Wiltshire, 85 miles (135 km) from London.

Stonehenge was built in three phases: first, as a timber circle enclosed by a ditch; second, as a ring of bluestones brought 245 miles (380 km) from Wales; and third, with the addition of an outer ring of giant standing stones. Stonehenge is an astronomical observatory marking the rising of the sun, moon, and stars. On Midsummer's Day, the stones forming the main entrance of the outer circle frame the rising sun.

✳ Stonehenge is just one of the many ancient monuments to discover in Wiltshire. Just under 2 miles (3 km) north of Stonehenge is Woodhenge, dated to 2300 B.C.E., which once comprised six rings of wooden posts.

✳ North of Salisbury, Avesbury has a mile-long avenue of standing stones and two giant stone circles, the largest of which consists of 100 stones.

✳ The nearby West Kennet Long Barrow originally consisted of a burial mound 330 feet (110 m) long formed around a core of great boulders. At the eastern end of the mound there is an elaborate structure with five chambers opening off a central passage, which contained the remains of 46 ancient Britons.

✳ Traditionally the most ancient Christian sanctuary in England and the legendary burial place for King Arthur, Glastonbury Abbey, Somerset, is 117 miles (189 km)

WHEN TO VISIT

See p.77 for general remarks on the British weather, which hold true for the southwest of England. The busiest time of year at Stonehenge are the days around the summer solstice, when the New Pagans of Britain, followers of Wicca, and New Age druids and travelers congregate at the stones to celebrate one of the high days and holidays of the Celtic year. During the 1990s, Stonehenge was the site of violent confrontations between the police and the New Age visitors over southwest of London. The abbey, once an important pilgrimage center, was forced to close when Henry VIII abolished all the monastic institutions in England in the sixteenth century. Its magnificent ruins are set in 36 acres (14.5 ha) of parkland. One of the ancient traditions that made the abbey famous was that is the site of the fabled Isle of Avalon and the resting place of King Arthur and his queen. In the twelfth century, the monks unearthed an ancient tomb on the grounds of the abbey on which was inscribed, "Here lies buried the renowned King Arthur with Guinevere, his second wife, in the Isle of Avalon." Another legend tells that Joseph of Arimathea came to Glastonbury after the crucifixion of Jesus Christ, bringing with him the Holy Grail, the cup that contained the blood of Christ.

∗ Once the site of an Iron Age fort built by the Anglo-Saxons, Glastonbury Tor rises dramatically from the flat Somerset countryside to a height of 525 feet (158 m), giving unrivaled views of the surrounding countryside.

Sacred place of power, astronomical observatory, or solar temple: the mystery of Stonehenge remains unsolved.

access to the site, leading to pitched battles. However, the situation has since eased, and the authorities have allowed controlled access to the site during the solstice celebrations. In addition to the ruins of the abbey, Glastonbury is famous for its annual international music festival held in June at Worthy Farm, in the village of Shepton Mallet. The event, which features top bands from the world over, attracts many thousands of visitors.

The Mountain of Heaven

MOUNT FUJI, JAPAN

The perfect snow-covered cone of Mount Fuji has long been the symbol of Japan. The trail that winds its way to the summit is thronged by pilgrims of all ages, who make the arduous climb at night so that they can witness the rising of the sun from its summit.

WHERE

West of the Japanese capital, Tokyo, which means "eastern capital" to differentiate it from the ancient capital of Kyoto in western Japan (see p.118), rises Japan's holy mountain, Mount Fuji, Fujiyama or Fujisan in Japanese. Climbing Mount Fuji, though it was never a religious duty for the Japanese, has for centuries been a popular pilgrimage for those who want to witness the sunrise from its summit. The all-night climb is far from being a gentle stroll, but the views that will reward the visitor are well worth the effort. Less arduous trails crisscross the area around the mountain, the Fuji-Hakone-Izu National Park, leading to the temples, shrines, and monasteries that have been built in its shadow. Although your spirit will be uplifted by the majesty of the mountain, your

body will be weary from your exertions, and ready to sink into the warm embrace of one of the many *onsen*, or natural hot spring resorts, to be found in the region.

"As time goes on, he becomes an infatuating personality."
Isabella Bird on Mount Fuji, 1880

LOCAL KNOWLEDGE

The weather on Mount Fuji is unpredictable at any time of the year. Even at the height of summer, temperatures can fall to freezing, so you should come equipped for any eventuality. The Japanese authorities recommend that you pack the following equipment to climb the mountain: sturdy hiking boots; waterproof jackets; layered clothing that you can put on and remove as necessary; a flashlight (if climbing at night); sunglasses and sunscreen for the descent the next day; 1 to 2 liters of water (2-4 pints); some high-energy bars and a packed meal (*obento* in Japanese); and, finally, they list, toilet paper (public restrooms in Japan rarely have toilet paper). Very basic accommodation huts are strategically placed all over the mountain, but you will have to pay an hourly charge to rest there.

Made famous by hundreds of woodblock prints, posters, postage stamps, and postcards, the perfect volcanic cone of Mount Fuji rises above the waters of Lake Ashinoko.

WHAT TO DO

✳ At 12,385 feet (3,776 m), Mount Fuji is not only Japan's best-known landmark, it is also its highest mountain. Still listed as an active volcano on this island on the Pacific "Ring of Fire," Fujisan last blew its top in 1707, covering Tokyo, just 62 miles (99 km) away, in a coating of fine gray ash. Allow between five and eight hours for the ascent, and another three to four for the descent.

✳ The most popular route starts at Kawaguchiko Fifth Station (alt. 7,562 feet/2,305 m), which is the last place you can buy supplies until the summit. The climb starts in green pastures but the scenery quickly changes to barren volcanic fields strewn with jagged rocks. You reach the summit by passing through a Shinto shrine gate, or *torii*, and thus entering a sacred space. However, this is Japan, and you will also find accommodation huts, and shops selling souvenirs, drinks, and light meals to fortify you for your return journey. A complete circuit of the active, smoking crater takes about one hour.

✳ There are several alternative routes to climb the mountain, via Subashiri, Fujinomiya, and the longest (and hardest) from Gotemba, which crosses a long stretch of volcanic sand.

✳ The Fuji-Hakone-Izu National Park that fringes Lake Ashinoko, is a popular attraction well known for its hiking trails, hot spring resorts, or *onsen*, and, of course, for unrivaled views of Mount Fuji.

✳ The Great Boiling Valley is a volcanic hotspot full of sulfurous springs that can be reached by cable car from Sounzan.

✳ Hakone Jinja, nestling on the southern shore of Lake Ashinoko, is a picturesque Shinto shrine whose gate, or *torii*, stands in the waters of the lake.

✳ A good way to relax after climbing Mount Fuji or hiking in the national park is to bathe in the naturally heated, mineral-rich waters of the region, which is home to the "Hakone *juschichitoh*," the "17 Famous Hakone Hot Springs." Many of the springs cater to the day tripper, and you can soak away the grime and your aches and pains in the outdoor pools for a small fee before catching your train or bus back to Tokyo.

✳ A far more agreeable way to "take the waters" Japanese-style is to stay at an *onsen ryokan*, a traditional inn with its own hot spring. If you are going for this option, go for the smaller family-run establishments, usually to be found a little outside the main resorts, where you can sample Japanese hospitality at its best. The all-inclusive price will include your *tatami*-mat room, indoor and outdoor *onsen* facilities, a lavish Japanese evening meal, and a hearty Japanese breakfast of rice, Japanese pickles, and fish.

WHEN TO VISIT

The climbing season is limited to July and August because of the obvious dangers of climbing the mountain at other times of year. If you are visiting the Fuji-Hakone-Izu National Park to hike and sightsee, the most pleasant times of year are spring and fall. Summers can be stifling with high humidity. A winter trip to the area can be the best time to appreciate the joys of the local *onsen*, when you can sit in the warmth of an outdoor *rotemburo* hot spring pool, and gaze up at the snow-capped perfection of the great mountain towering above you while sipping a cup of warm *sake*—heaven indeed!

One of the most relaxing activities you can experience in Japan is a stay at a traditional "onsen" or hot spring resort. Many such springs can be found near Mount Fuji, although naturally occurring coastal onsens, as shown here, are also common.

Good fresh local produce and traditional cooking methods combine to produce dishes that are both delicious and healthy.

GASTRONOMIC GETAWAY

Conviviality and good cheer are popular with everyone but, nowadays, diet and health are also major concerns. These gourmet excursions will teach you the secrets of how to live both well and long. Red wine is now recognized to have many benefits—where better to sample this delicious tonic than in France's most-famous wine-producing region? The Thai and Mediterranean diets are recommended as the best for our hearts—learn how to cook them in the country of their origin, or discover the ultimate in "New Age" cuisine in a Japanese Zen monastery.

The World's Best Medicine

BORDEAUX WINE REGION, FRANCE

An old French saying holds that a glass of good red wine is the only doctor that anyone will ever need. This story probably began in France's premier wine region of Bordeaux. Wine has been made here since the days of the Romans and continues to be, using traditional methods in the area's many chateaux.

"Bordeaux is dedicated to the worship of Bacchus in the most discreet form." Henry James, 1882

France's largest wine-producing region, Bordeaux is famous for it's "appelation" vintages of red, white, and rosé wines.

The elegant neoclassical city of Bordeaux, built on the banks of the river Garonne, has grown rich on its association with the international wine trade.

WHERE

The capital of the ancient region of Aquitaine, Bordeaux, on the river Garonne, is a city of grand eighteenth-century architecture, 362 miles (579 km) southwest of Paris, with good road, rail, and air links to all major French destinations. Once the jealously guarded possession of the English kings, and fought over in many wars between England and France, the Bordelais is the largest and best-known wine-producing region of France, home to some of the world's most illustrious and sought-after wines. The city is surrounded by great wine-producing estates: the famous *grands chateaux* (though they do not always come with an actual castle), most of which operate wine-tasting tours for visitors. The wines of the region are divided into six categories: four reds and two whites. The Médoc and Graves reds include such famous *appellations* as St-Estèphe, Pauillac, and Margaux; the Libourne region includes St-Emilion, Pomerol, and Fronsac; and the remaining reds fall under the Bordeaux or Côte *appellations*. Whites are divided into dry *appellations*, including Graves and Entre-Deux-Mers, and sweet dessert wines, including the delicious Sauternes.

WHAT TO DO

With 295,000 acres of vines, the Bordeaux wine region is the largest in France. It produces a huge range of vintages, with no less than 57 *appellations*, wines whose names are protected by law to maintain their quality. The region has been divided into several *routes* (roads), which cover the main wine-producing areas and their attractions.

✶ *La route des chateaux* (northwest—Médoc)

On the Chateaux Road you will sample the world's best-known vintages—the *Grands Crus Classés* of 1855, and see the region's most spectacular architecture, including the Palladian splendor that is Chateau Margaux.

✶ *La route des coteaux* (north—Bourg, Blaye)

This follows the Gironde estuary, home of full-bodied, fruity wines grown in the shadow of picturesque villages. The seventeenth-century fortress of Blaye is a great place to view the surrounding countryside and sit down to a gastronomic banquet accompanied by the area's wines.

✶ *La route du patrimoine* (east—Saint-Emilion, Pomerol, Fronsac)

The Heritage Road boasts many wines with international reputations. The village of Saint-Emilion is built over some 125 miles (200 km) of underground tunnels in which the famous vintages are stored and aged to perfection.

✶ *La route des bastides* (southeast—Entre-Deux-Mers)

The area "between the two seas," meaning the two rivers, Garonne and Dordogne, produces fresh, crisp wines made to be drunk "young." This is a great area to find lodgings to experience the region's famed gastronomy and hospitality.

✶ *La route des Graves* (southwest—Graves, Sauternes)

Bordering the Landaise forest, the area is home to a variety of wines, including reds, whites, and fortified dessert wines.

LOCAL KNOWLEDGE

Unlike Australian and U.S. wines that are labeled by grape variety (e.g., Shiraz, Merlot, or Chardonnay), in France, labels traditionally display only the name of the producer and the area of production by which the wine is known. The major red grape varieties of Bordeaux are Cabernet Sauvignon, Merlot, and Cabernet Franc, with the addition of small quantities of Malbec, Petit Verdot, and Carmenère for balance. The white wines use mainly Sauvignon Blanc and Sémillon varieties.

WHEN TO VISIT

France is a country of varied climatic zones. The far south, the Côte d'Azure, has a very warm, dry climate, while the northern

* The interactive Wine Ecomuseum (*Ecomusée de la vigne et du vin*) in the village of Gradignan, 3 miles (5 km) from Bordeaux town center, is housed in a typical nineteenth-century "*maisons de vigneron*" (winemaker's house), where you can learn the art of winemaking and taste some of its products.

* Take a course at the prestigious Bordeaux Wine School. The school offers a variety of wine-appreciation courses for the visitor, from the basic two-hour course to one-day and weekend courses, with visits to some of the area's best-known *chateaux* for on-site "*dégustations*" (tastings).

The yearly Bordeaux "vendanges" (grape-picking season) begins in September.

region is much closer to the U.K. and Holland with colder winters and rain. The western part of the country, which includes Bordeaux, has a maritime climate, which has more humid, cooler summers than the Mediterranean coast. Expect warm to hot summers and mild, cool winters on your trip to the vineyards. A highlight of the Bordeaux year is the *vendanges* (grape harvest) season in the fall. The month of August is the traditional vacation month in France, and though fewer people take the whole month off these days, this is the busiest month for the coastal resorts. If driving, avoid the rush to the coasts around the beginning of August, and the rush back to work at the end of the month.

Feasting in the Land of Smiles

CHIANG MAI, NORTHWESTERN THAILAND

From the elegant riverside restaurants and street stalls of Bangkok, to the floating cafés of Thai's river markets and the cookery schools of Chiang Mai, Thai cuisine's subtle tastes and variety always surprise and keeps visitors coming back for more.

WHERE

The thirteenth-century city of Chiang Mai, known as the "Rose of the North" because of the abundance of flowers that grow in its temperate climate, is in the northwestern part of Thailand, which borders Myanmar (Burma) to the west and Laos to the east. The capital of an independent state in medieval times, Chiang Mai is now a major regional tourist center, with a host of activities including guided visits to the neighboring hill tribes and elephant trekking along forest trails. The old town is a partially walled moated square, whose streets are lined with ancient buildings, monasteries, and soaring temple spires. A modern town, the second largest in Thailand, with good transport, accommodations, dining, and shopping facilities, has grown up alongside the old city. An increasingly popular draw to the city are the Thai cooking schools that have opened there, offering authentic training in the subtle flavors of Thai cooking in the land of their origin.

The untamed country around Chiang Mai is ideal for adventurous forest hikes, river rafting, and elephant safaris.

WHAT TO DO

✳ A dozen or so cooking schools have opened in and around Chiang Mai (see reference section for details, p.142), with courses in the classic dishes of Thailand, regional specialties, as well as vegetarian cooking. The courses are held in family-style kitchens that combine traditional methods, ingredients, and equipment with western conveniences. Courses range from a half-day introduction to intensive three-day courses, with ingredient shopping at the local markets. One school offers tuition in a village outside the city, with accommodations provided in traditional bamboo bungalows.

✳ One of the holiest shrines in Thailand, and an important Buddhist pilgrimage center, the sixteenth-century Wat Phra Borommathat Temple overlooks the city from the summit of Doi Suthep (3,520 feet/1,072 m), 10 miles (16 km) from Chiang Mai. You can reach the temple by a 290-step climb, or less energetically but just as scenically, by the cable car.

✳ The surrounding Doi Inthanon Park offers good hiking along forest tracks with views over the surrounding country, but the trails are not well marked, and you should take advice from the park rangers if you are intending to hike the more isolated areas.

✳ If you saw the movie, *The King and I,* you will recall the scene when a white elephant is born in the country, a sign of great good fortune for the kingdom. Well into the twentieth century, elephants were the tractors, trucks, and forklifts of the forest. Now mostly retired from their work duties, elephants take part in shows and safaris. Nineteen miles (30 km) from Chiang Mai is the Mae Sa Elephant Camp, from where you can take a two-hour elephant ride after the show. The riverside Taeng Doa Elephant Camp, 35 miles (56 km) from the city offers river-rafting as well as elephant shows and rides, and visits to the local hill tribe villages.

Once the "pickup truck" of the jungle, the elephant has now been retrained for tourism

THAI CUISINE

The popularity of Thai food has soared in the past decades, and with good reason. Not only is it extremely varied, fresh, and subtly flavored, it is also recognized as being among one of the world's lightest and healthiest culinary traditions, without deep-fried fatty foods, or heavy calorie-rich sauces. Central to Thai cooking is the search for a harmony of tastes, balancing a medley of sweet, sour, and spicy flavors. Typical ingredients include peanuts and coconut milk, as well as spices such as lemongrass, kaffir lime, both leaf and fruit, and galangal, a type of ginger. The Thais use a range of cooking techniques; meats and seafood are grilled and eaten with sweet-and-sour dips (*Nam Phrik*). Another popular technique is *yam*, or Thai salad. *Yam* is different from western salad because its dressing is not made with oil or mayo, and is therefore a lot lighter on the waistline. To dress a salad *yam* style, mix fish sauce, lemon juice, and chili, and sprinkle with garlic or shallots. Boiling is another popular and healthy way to prepare food—and not necessarily a bland one. Before the age of modern cooking appliances, the Thais cooked their food over open fires in clay pots, which they still use today to prepare rice and soups, such as the spicy *Tom-Yam-Gong* (spicy prawn soup). Thailand's trademark green and red curries have also changed since ancient times, with the addition of coconut milk that gives them their sweetness and creamy consistency. Chinese immigrants introduced stir-frying to Thailand, as well as noodle dishes. However, while the Chinese deep-fry noodles and season them with savory sauces, Thai noodles are served sweet, sour, or sometimes spicy. A distinctive local dish is *Mee Krob*, (crispy noodles). Last but not least, they make delicious desserts, such as *Khao-Neow-Ma-Maung*, a concoction of sticky rice, mangoes, and coconut milk.

WHEN TO VISIT

Thailand lies within the tropical monsoon zone of Southeast Asia, and enjoys a warm climate throughout the year. There are three seasons: cool (November through February), which is the most popular with visitors; hot (April–May) when temperatures can soar to 95°F (35°C), and rainy (June through October), during which some areas of the country will be difficult to access because of flooding. Evenings in the northern region around Chiang Mai can be cold enough to need a sweater and light jacket in the cool season.

The Middle Way to Health

LEARN MEDITERRANEAN COOKING IN SICILY

To stay youthful and healthy, doctors tell us that we should follow the Mediterranean diet. Where better to learn its secrets than on the enchanted island of Sicily in the middle of Europe's inland sea? Sicily, which has been in turn, Greek, Roman, Byzantine, Arab, Norman, Spanish, and Italian, is a cultural and culinary melting pot.

One of the gems of Sicily's eastern coastline, the city of Taormina, nestling beneath Mount Etna, has a history dating back to the Graeco-Roman period.

SICILIAN FOOD

Sicilian cooking is a heady blend of the cuisines of the different cultures that have ruled the island, overlaid with the classic dishes of Italy. The Greek Miteco is said to have written the West's first cooking book here five centuries before our era, sadly now lost. It was the ancient Greeks who discovered the island's potential for growing olives, fruit, vegetables, and wheat, and made the first honey and cheeses. The Romans imported the vine, beginning a winemaking tradition that flourishes to this day. The Arabs brought with them the cultivation of the orange, lemon, eggplant, sugarcane, and rice, and introduced the use of cinnamon and candied fruit. One of the island's richest cooking traditions is to be found in Catania south of Taormina on the east coast, which specializes in seafood dishes—try the *insalata di mare* (seafood salad) and the *maculi marinati* (anchovies marinated in olive oil and lemon), a trademark pasta dish, *pasta alla Norma*, (a tomato sauce with fried eggplants, basil, and ricotta cheese), and candy good enough for the sweetest tooth made from Sicily's other great gift to the world, marzipan.

Quality ingredients is one of the secrets of Sicilian cooking.

WHERE

The mountainous island of Sicily is the football that the "boot" of Italy is kicking toward North America, which seems appropriate given how many immigrants from Sicily have made their way to American shores. The island has one of Europe's most active volcanoes, Mount Etna (10,902 feet/3,323 m), and is surrounded by a scattering of unspoiled islands and archipelagos: the isles of Eolie, Egadi, Pelagie, Pantelleria, and Ustica. Forming a bridge between Europe and Africa, Sicily has always been a cultural crossroads.

Colonized by the ancient Greeks, who christened it Magna Grecia (Greater Greece), it boasts many ruins dating back to Greek and Roman times. Subsequent overlords included the Byzantines, the Arabs, the Normans, and the Spanish, who each left their architectural, cultural, culinary, and linguistic legacies to modern Sicily. A province of Italy since the country's reunification in the nineteenth century, Sicily is now a popular vacation destination with both Italians and northern Europeans.

WHAT TO DO

✻ The three pillars of Italian life are the Church, the family, and last, but not least, good food. Unlike northern Europeans, who often display a utilitarian approach to eating, Italians love to spend time discussing food, preparing it, and savoring it. Given the choice, they will sit down to two four-course meals a day, and it is a testament to the healthful qualities of the Mediterranean diet that they have one of the lowest adult obesity rates in the developed world.

✻ Schools on the island offer a range of courses on Sicilian and Italian cooking and wine appreciation. These are run in the island's larger towns, small villages, or secluded resorts, to suit every preference and budget.

✻ The Cucina del Sole cooking school is in the village of Viagrande on the slopes of Mount Etna. The courses are held in an eighteenth-century Sicilian house, and have a relaxed family atmosphere. The area is famous for its orchards and market gardens, fragrant with orange and lemon groves, vineyards, and pistachio and olive groves, which produce the trademark products used in the local cuisine.

✻ The ancient Greek town of Taormina on the east coast of Sicily is perched 650 feet (200 m) above the deep blue Mediterranean Sea, with unrivaled views of Mount Etna at the back and over the Straits of Messina and the Italian mainland beyond. Its winding streets, unchanged since the Middle Ages, are filled with the color and scent of flowers in spring.

✻ An enterprising language school in Taormina (see reference section for details) organizes cooking lessons with a real Sicilian "*mamma*" in her kitchen, where she takes you through a full Sicilian meal from pasta to dessert.

✻ Or you could study in the kitchens of one of Taormina's restaurants, the Casa Grugno, where you will learn the chef's unique fusion style of modern Italian and traditional Sicilian cuisines.

✻ The island is famous for its regional wines, cheeses, and olive oils, and local producers offer guided visits with tastings, as well as *agriturismo* (farm homestays), which are a popular alternative to staying in hotels, and provide an ideal opportunity to observe how a Sicilian family cooks and eats at first hand.

"Taormina should be let out by the Italian government, as an open-air asylum for Anglo-Saxons who live by the adage that 'time is money.'...Nobody ever looks at a clock in Taormina."
Walter Starkie, 1938

Sicily produces a wide range of specialty produce, including the island's trademark oils, which are pressed from the local olives.

WHEN TO VISIT

Sicily is too large an island to suffer from the depredations that afflict smaller Mediterranean island resorts, such as Corfu and Ibiza, which are swamped by the huge numbers of visitors they accommodate in the summer months. However, with many attractions, resorts, and beaches, it does attract a flock of sun seekers during the peak European summer season (July–August), when the temperature can soar into the 90s°F (30s°C). Far more agreeable (and cooler) times to visit the island are spring (April–May) and fall (October–November).

A Feast for the Spirit

ZEN CUISINE IN KYOTO, JAPAN

Originally reserved for monks training in Zen Buddhism, "shojin ryori" is now available to the visitor. Served in the tranquil surroundings of Kyoto's Zen temples and traditional inns, "shojin ryori" consists of a vegetarian banquet of beautifully presented, delicately flavored dishes, providing nourishment for mind, body, and spirit.

WHERE

Far from the hustle and bustle of Japan's ultramodern capital, Tokyo, Kyoto in the Kinki region of western Japan, is an urban jewel box of architectural treasures that have survived thirteen centuries of man-made and natural calamities. Kyoto was Japan's capital from 794 to 1867, and its imperial past is written large on its neatly planned grid of streets. The Go-Sho—the Imperial Palace and its landscaped park—occupies the center of the city, and you will discover castles, villas, Shinto shrines, temples, monasteries, and mausoleums liberally scattered among its streets and suburbs. Kyoto is very much a city of tradition—in architecture, dress, lifestyle, and food, and behind the sliding paper doors of its traditional inns and teahouses, you will find exquisitely presented delicacies that look far too good to eat. An ancient culinary tradition of the city known as *shojin ryori* was inspired by the austere vegetarian diet of Zen Buddhist monks.

"There is a saying that the Chinese eat with their stomachs and the Japanese with their eyes."
Bernard Leach, 1960

The austere aesthetic principles of Zen Buddhism known as "wabi" and "sabi" have influenced every aspect of Japanese cultural and artistic life.

LOCAL KNOWLEDGE

Shojin ryori was originally served to monks in large metal bowls known as *teppatsu*. As the sect became more popular, laymen began to visit the temples for meals and brought back vegetarian recipes to their homes. In a traditional setting, you are served *shojin ryori* from a *honzen*, a low tray on legs, while sitting on a cushion on a *tatami* mat floor. *Shojin ryori* is also served during the *chanoyu* (tea ceremony), and is the basis for *kaiseki ryori*, the food eaten on formal occasions in

Japan. Typical ingredients include different types of tofu (soybean curd), *natto* (fermented soybeans), *konyaku* (strips made from the starch of rum root), different types of seaweed, including *konbu* (kelp), *wakame* (seagreens), *arame*, *hijiki*, and *nori*, as well as many kinds of vegetables, mushrooms, roots, fruits, and nuts. Although the dishes are all vegetarian, such is the artistry of *shojin ryori* that you are often fooled into thinking that you are eating fish or meat.

WHEN TO VISIT

Kyoto, like Tokyo (see p.100), has four well-defined seasons with a rainy season lasting from mid-June to mid-July. Once the rains have passed, the summers are extremely warm and humid. Winters are cold but with clear blue skies. The most pleasant seasons are spring and fall, known respectively for cherry blossom viewing on the Kamo River, and for excursions to see the changing colors of foliage in the surrounding countryside.

WHAT TO DO

✳ Large Zen temples in Japan are multipurpose complexes. There are the religious buildings—the lecture and Buddha halls, containing cult statues—but because Zen is a religion without rituals and ceremonies, the real work goes on in the surrounding small subtemples, which are residential and teaching centers.

✳ Daitokuji in northwestern Kyoto is one of Japan's great Zen centers. A large, quiet walled complex, it lacks the crowds of pilgrims, the golden Buddhas, clouds of incense, gongs, and ritual chants of other sects. The main halls are scrupulously clean but shuttered and unused. The real work goes on in Daitokuji's many subtemples, which look like traditional single-story Japanese houses with *tatami*-mat floors, paper wall partitions, and ancient gardens.

✳ One of Daitokuji's subtemples, Daiji-in, is home to a branch of the Izusen restaurant that specializes in *shojin ryori*. The meals are served in the main room of the temple with tranquil views over its garden, or *al fresco* in good weather.

✳ A cultural and gastronomic excursion not to be missed is the walk from Yasaka Shrine to the spectacular Kiyomizudera Temple that overlooks the city from atop a wooden platform, along the sloping paved roads known as Sannenzaka and Ninenzaka, which are lined with ancient wooden buildings housing craft shops and teahouses, serving delicate pastries made in the shape of seasonal fruits and flowers.

✳ For an echo of the life described in James Clavell's *Shogun*, take a tour of the Gion neighborhood near Yasaka Shrine. This is the old

KYOTO, CITY OF FESTIVALS

The city of Kyoto has a yearlong calendar of historical and cultural events. Among the highlights are the Aoi, Gion, Jidai, and O-Bon *matsuri* (festivals). The age-old Aoi Masturi (Hollyhock Festival), held on May 15 features a procession in historical costumes through the city. A similar event takes place on October 22, the Jidai Matsuri (Historical Festival). But the most extraordinary festivals take place in July and August: the month long Gion Matsuri, which culminates in a procession of 32 lavishly decorated *yama* and *hoko* floats dating back to the Medieval period. Teams of young people pull the gigantic *hoko* floats through the streets. In mid-August, the Buddhist festival of the dead, O-Bon, is celebrated with street parties, and the lighting of bonfires on the hills around the city in the shape of giant Chinese characters.

entertainment quarter of Kyoto whose streets are lined with restaurants and teahouses. In the past, many of these establishments provided a special kind of "entertainment" for gentlemen, and were the home to courtesans known to the West as *geisha*. Nowadays, Kyoto's very respectable *maiko*—entertainers trained in the traditional cultural accomplishments of eighteenth-century courtesans (music, dancing, and witty repartee) can be seen outfitted in their lavish silk kimonos, ebony-black hair coiffed to perfection, and faces made up in livid white, leaving for highly paid corporate entertaining engagements in private rooms in the local restaurants.

The Daitokuji temple complex in northwestern Kyoto is one of Japan's greatest Buddhist centers.

The best shopping experiences combine the modern conveniences
of malls with the traditional pleasures of open-air markets.

CONSUMER PARADISE

Humans have traded to survive
since time immemorial, but shopping
is now one of the world's favorite
pastimes. Experience the variety of the
world's shopping opportunities on
these consumer excursions; once the
caravans of Arabia used to set off from
this desert kingdom; now the buyers
flock in by air. Discover the most chic
couture in the capitals of European
fashion; whatever you want to buy,
you will find it as the Far East's world
emporia of Hong Kong or Singapore.
Or, for a change of pace, sample the
wares on sale in the Great Bazaar
of the city that stands between
East and West.

Golden Touch

Dubai

In ancient myth, King Croesus's touch turned everything to gold, but in the modern world, it is the merchants of Dubai who have inherited his talent. For millennia an important trading port, Dubai now boasts some of the world's most impressively modern vacation and shopping facilities.

WHERE

The Middle East has not had good press in recent years, but that doesn't mean you should rule out the region as a travel destination. The United Arab Emirates (UAE), a federation of small states on the south coast of the Persian Gulf, has always welcomed overseas visitors and have a long tradition of generous hospitality. In 1966, the seven emirates of the UAE struck "black gold," which initiated their transformation from sleepy desert backwaters into some of the richest and most dynamic nations on earth. Forty years later, Dubai, with its liberal *laissez-faire* economic and social policies, offers a beguiling mixture of Arab tradition, with Bedouin villages around desert oases and camel races, and cutting-edge twenty-

first-century infrastructure, with superhighways, artificial islands, and gleaming landmark buildings. Trade has always been the lifeblood of Dubai, and today, the shopper can sample the age-old customs of bargaining in the *souks*, as well as enjoying the air-conditioned comfort of some of the world's best-appointed malls.

LOCAL KNOWLEDGE

Western visitors should be aware of several cultural differences when visiting an Islamic country. Although Dubai does not ban alcohol as several of its more conservative neighbors do, it follows Islamic custom for the weekly day of rest, which is Friday and not Sunday, making the Dubai weekend, Thursday and Friday. Ramadan is the yearly month-long fast prescribed by Islam. As the dates of Ramadan are set according to the lunar calendar, it is a movable fast. The rules for Ramadan are simple: believers abstain from food and drink of any kind (as well as tobacco and sexual intercourse) from sunup to sunset; and evening signals a stampede to the local cafés and eateries. Naturally, food and drink will be available in resorts and hotels, but restaurants and cafés in the souks will be closed, and you should be careful not to offend the locals by any conspicuous consumption of food, drinks, and tobacco products during fast days (conspicuous consumption of the local merchandise, however, is always welcome!).

The extraordinary futuristic skyline that has transformed Dubai into the Manhattan of the Gulf has sprung up in the last few decades after the discovery of "black gold" in the region.

WHAT TO DO

∗ Visitors to Dubai have two options to choose from or combine, as they prefer. There is the old Dubai of the desert, the archeological past, the traditional covered markets, or *souks*, and the modern Dubai of shopping malls, high-rise hotels, golf courses, and beach resorts.

∗ The symbol of the new Dubai is the striking Burj Al Arab (Arabian Tower) Hotel. The world's tallest hotel (and possibly, its most expensive and luxurious) is built in the shape of the sail of a traditional Arab sailing ship, or dhow. Standing on an artificial island, the Burj Al Arab is just one of the many skyscrapers that have transformed Dubai into the Manhattan of the Gulf.

∗ With more than 30 state-of-the-art shopping centers and malls, Dubai is a shopaholic's dream. The emirate hosts two major bargain bonanzas during the year: the Dubai Shopping Festival (mid-January through mid-February), and the Dubai Summer Surprises (in June).

∗ Modern Dubai's fortunes may be built on "black gold," but in days of yore, it was yellow gold, earned in trade, that made its merchants rich. Today, Dubai still has many traditional covered markets, or *souks*, selling everything from gold to silk, fish, and spices. The Gold *Souk* is the largest emporium of gold and precious metals in Arabia, and will dazzle even the most jaded visitor with the luster of

WHEN TO VISIT

The coolest months to visit the desert emirate of Dubai are January and February, when temperatures top out at a comfortable 73°F (23°C), with nights a pleasant 66°F (19°C); the hottest are June through September, when daytime temperatures reach 100°F (38°C) during the day, and hover around a sticky 89°F (32°C) at night. Desert heat, however, is dry heat, and with the sea nearby, is a lot easier to handle than the humid heat of the tropics.

its wares. More modest, and accessible buys can be made at the Meena Bazaar, which sells silk and cotton wares. Other markets worth a visit are the spice *souk*, with its aromatic cargoes of cloves, cinnamon, and cardamoms; the more pungent fish *souk*; and the perfume *souk*, which sells both Western and Eastern fragrances.

✳ In Dubai, the romance of the desert is only a short SUV ride away. Here you will find the same intriguing mix of ancient and modern pastimes: visiting a Bedouin village, where you can learn to ride a camel or feast under the stars, and at the other extreme, you can try dune driving, "wadi-bashing" (racing along dry riverbeds), or sand skiing.

✳ For those with less extreme sporting tastes, Dubai has several world-class golf courses, including two that regularly host the PGA tour; the Naad Al Sheba Race Course, which hosts the world's richest horse race, the Dubai World Cup; and a stunning palm-fringed beach and picnic area at the Jumeirah Park.

Away from the city high-rises, traditional life continues in Bedouin villages.

Shopping à la Mode

Paris and Milan are the twin fashion hubs of the world. Home to the biggest and brightest stars of the fashion firmament, and the backdrops for the twice-yearly spectacle of the "prêt-à-porter" (ready-to-wear) and "haute-couture" collections, these two cities are the epitome of European elegance.

WHERE

Paris, the "City of Lights," capital of fashion, romance, and *gastronomie,* needs little introduction, but Milan, northern Italy's industrial and commercial heart, is less well known. Milan was a major Roman city in Antiquity, a leading city-state during the Renaissance, and it continued to develop over the centuries with many architectural and cultural additions, including a gleaming white marble wedding-cake Duomo (cathedral) and the extravagant Galleria Vittorio Emanuele. The modern city owes its broad avenues and

At the heart of Milan stands the extraordinary Galleria Vittorio Emanuele.

apartment blocks to the urban planning of the 1930s. Every winter, the world's "fashionista"—magazine editors, store buyers, photographers, supermodels, celebrities, and assorted hangers-on—go on a breakneck tour of the world's fashion capitals, starting in New York, taking in London and Milan, and finishing in Paris, where they are fêted and feasted by fashion houses that present their latest collections at strictly invitation-only catwalk shows. During the shows, Paris and Milan's designer outlets and department stores go into overdrive in a fashion-feeding frenzy.

LOCAL KNOWLEDGE

In Paris, the catwalk shows are held at the Carousel du Louvre (outside the Louvre Museum), and in Milan, at the Fiera Milano. The shows are strictly invitation-only, and unless you are well connected in the world of fashion, the closest you will get to them and their celebrity audiences is behind the barriers that line the red carpet. With the invited audience of buyers and journalists and models rushing from show to show, delays pile up, and by the afternoon, shows are running late, and it is not just the hems that are getting frayed. So, remember, if you are hoping to catch a glimpse of the stars, don't expect punctuality.

WHAT TO DO

* Visiting Paris and Milan during their Fashion Weeks might be your idea of shopping heaven or hell. On the downside, city-center hotels are full, and fashionable restaurants are booked, but on the upside, the two cities are abuzz with fashion gossip, revelations, and drama, busy with special events; and teeming with celebrities.

* As you might imagine, Paris offers a dizzying range of shopping alternatives: the *haute couture* houses of the Faubourg Saint-Honoré and the Avenue Montaigne (8th *arrondissement*—the equivalent of a New York borough but much smaller) include Christian Dior,

Fashion houses like those on the Faubourg Saint-Honoré are not for the budget shopper.

Chanel, Christian Lacroix, and Yves Saint-Laurent Rive Gauche. Head for the rue du Cherche-Midi and rue de Grenelle (6th *arrondissement*) for high-quality leatherwear and accessories; trendsetters should take in Rue Etienne Marcel and Place des Victoires (1st and 2nd *arrondissements*).

* Now you have the dress, bag, and shoes, but for that all-important finishing touch, visit the jewelers on Paris's most expensive street, the Rue de la Paix (2nd *arrondissement*), where you will find jewelers Cartier, Boucheron, and Van Cleef and Arpels.

* If the offerings of the Rue de la Paix are a little beyond your pocketbook, take the métro to the Boulevard Haussman

(9th *arrondissement*) near the Opera House, where you will find the city's *grands magasins* (department stores), including the two great Paris rivals: the Printemps and the Galeries Lafayette. Other popular Paris department stores include the Bon Marché (7th *arrondissement*), La Samaritaine (1st *arrondissement*), and the BHV (4th *arrondissement*).

* The Italian city of Milan offers a very different shopping experience. While Paris oozes fashion tradition but can occasionally suffer from a slightly stuffy *hauteur*, Milan is slick, stylish, and utterly minimalist. For the very latest in Italian designer fashions, including Italy's big guns, Gucci, Prada, Armani, Moschino, Valentino, and Versace, lose yourself in the Quadrilatero d'Oro (Milan's shopping Bermuda Triangle), formed by the Via Montenapoleone,

Via Sant' Andrea, Via Borgospesso, and Via della Spiga, where the showrooms and shops are works of art in their own right.

* For more affordable but no less stylish shopping, investigate the Corso Vittorio Emanuele and Via Torino, and Milan's own historic department store La Rinascente next to the Duomo.

* A pitstop you should always plan on when visiting Milan is the nineteenth-century cast-iron and glass extravaganza, the Galleria Vittorio Emanuele, a 640 feet (195 m) domed passageway lined with shops and cafés that links the Piazza de la Scala and the Piazza del Duomo. Legend has it that stepping on a certain "part" of the *tauro* (bull) depicted on the ornate mosaic floor will bring you good fortune.

WHEN TO VISIT

There are several fashion weeks during the year: the *prêt-à-porter* (ready-to-wear) collections of the all-important spring-summer wear take place in February and March, but there are also the fall-winter collections, the *haute couture* collections, and the menswear shows. The French and northern Italian winter can see very chilly temperatures, with snow and ice, but there can also be glorious clear, crisp sunny days; rain or shine, you will need to bring your winter wardrobe (and make sure it is this season's!). And if you are planning your trip during Fashion Week, make sure you book your hotel well in advance.

Eastern Promises

HONG KONG AND SINGAPORE

Whether it's the latest digital camera, a Prada bag, or a fine Scottish malt, you are likely to find them all in the world's greatest shopping emporia, Singapore and Hong Kong. These two former British colonies were built on trade and continue to thrive on it.

WHERE

"Go west, young man," so the saying goes, but if it's the shopping experience of a lifetime you're after, it is eastward that you should turn. If it is for sale anywhere in the world, you will find it in Hong Kong and Singapore, the two main financial and commercial centers of Asia. Territorially insignificant, these two city-states bat way over their size in the world's economic ballgame. Both Hong Kong, "Fragrant Harbor," and Singapore, "the City of the Lion," were sleepy fishing communities before the British arrived. In Singapore, it was the famous Sir Stamford Raffles who first discovered and exploited the city's extraordinary trading potential. The Republic of Singapore is a multicultural melting pot of cultures: Chinese, Arab, British, Malaysian, and Indian. Hong Kong, which reverted to Chinese control in 1997, retains its status as a semiautonomous region within the communist giant. But when strolling among its high-rise streets and luxury malls, thronged with couture-clad shoppers, you'd never dream that you are in the People's Republic of China.

LOCAL KNOWLEDGE

Bargain hunters should head to Singapore during the Great Singapore Sale held in June/July, when retailers all over the island compete in discounting their prices and offering special promotions. With the exception of department stores and Western-style boutiques, when shopping in either Hong Kong or Singapore you should haggle over prices. This does not come naturally to many Westerners who are used to paying what they are asked, but when you think that you could get goods at between 25 and 50 percent less than the asking price if you bargain, it's well worth the initial effort.

The ultramodern towers of banks and large corporations jostle for attention on the Hong Kong skyline, while at their feet you will discover the hustle and bustle of street markets.

WHAT TO DO

* Hong Kong is divided into four main areas: Hong Kong Island, the original heart of the British colony, with the famous Victoria Peak and harborside and its high-rise skyline; Kowloon, on the mainland, originally the Chinese trading district; the New Territories, the industrial and agricultural belt separating Hong Kong from China proper; and the islands in and around the harbor.

* If it's luxury you're after, you need go no further than Admiralty on Hong Kong Island, where you will find its smartest designer malls, including the spectacular Pacific Place.

* Hong Kong Island also has its traditional Chinese side, "The Lanes," Li Yuen Street East and West, with hundreds of stalls where bargains are to be had in clothing, watches, costume jewelry, luggage, and shoes.

* For antiques, head to Hollywood Road, which winds above "Central," Hong Kong's business district.

Walking west, toward Sheung Wan, you'll encounter crowds of sidewalk hawkers on Central's steeply sloping streets.

* Tsim Sha Tsui, Kowloon, is a compact area of shops, restaurants, and cultural attractions with good views across to Hong Kong Island. The busiest night market in Hong Kong is on Temple Street in Yau Ma Tai.

* Jade has a special place in Chinese culture because it is associated with long life and health. The stones sold as jade in Hong Kong are either true jade or jadeite. The Jade Market on Kansu and Battery streets in Yau Ma Tai has 400 stalls selling a wide range of jewelry, carvings, and ornaments. The best and most expensive jade is pure green. Cheaper pieces will have a yellow tinge, and the lowest quality (which the Chinese will not buy) has traces of brown or gray. The best jadeite is semitransparent, while stones showing cloudy patches are less valued.

* Every shopping area and mall in Hong Kong has its own anchor department store, including international names such as Marks & Spencer from the U.K., and SOGO from Japan; Wing On, Sincere, and Lane Crawford are Hong Kong's homegrown alternatives.

Since ancient times, the Chinese have been great maritime traders.

* Singapore is not the bargain hunter's dream it once was. Prices have been climbing steadily, while designer and electronic goods get cheaper back home, but for sheer choice, volume, and bargains, you still cannot beat a Singaporean shopping spree at bargain sale time.

* Orchard Road is synonymous with shopping in Singapore. Here you will find the city's major hotels, theaters, restaurants, and malls, malls, malls! For high-end stores and designer labels, head for the Palais Renaissance, the Paragon, and Ngee Ann City; the Far East Plaza caters to the younger, hipper crowd; shop for artwork and antiques at the Tanglin Shopping Centre, and for souvenirs from the Shaw Centre; the Centrepoint and renovated Plaza Singapura offer general shopping, and smaller malls specialize in sporting and electronic goods. All the malls have food courts and restaurants, but for a really varied selection, try the Tanglin Mall.

* Traditional shopping areas reflect Singapore's multicultural makeup: Arab Street, north of Beach Road features clothes, textiles, baskets, jewelry, and food outlets with a distinctly Islamic, Malaysian, Indonesian, or Arabic flavor; Chinatown was founded in the nineteenth century by Chinese merchants who traded cloth, medicine, gold, and foodstuffs; Little India sells gold, jewelry, clothing, textiles, spices, and Indian handicrafts.

Colonial elegance has been brought up to date at the restored Raffles Hotel.

WHEN TO VISIT

The winter months are the most pleasant in Hong Kong, with temperatures in the 70s°F (low 20s°C) and clear skies, so they will be the busiest for visitors, especially around Chinese New Year celebrations in January and February. From May to September, the rains begin and temperatures climb to the humid 80s°F (high 20s°C). Singapore has a more even climate, meaning that it is rather hot (highs around 86°F/30°C) and rainy all year, but the rain comes in the form of tropical downpours that quickly make way for brilliant sunshine.

In such a small place, an island with no natives, everyone a visitor, the foreigner made himself a resident by emphasizing his foreignness.
Paul Theroux, 1973

Turkish Delights

THE GRAND BAZAAR, ISTANBUL

Step back in time to another age of shopping and sample the wares of Istanbul's huge covered market, the Great Bazaar, a city within a city with its own manufactured goods, quarters, streets, squares, hotels, bathhouses, restaurants, and cafés.

WHERE

In ages past, the "Mysterious East" was said to begin at the gates of the mighty city of Constantinople, now known as Istanbul. The capital in turn of the Eastern Roman, Byzantine, and Ottoman empires, Istanbul is a city of architectural marvels dating back to Antiquity. Roman ruins, Byzantine churches, and Turkish mosques and palaces jostle for the visitor's attention in a fast-paced modern city with all the amenities you would expect from a major European capital. At the heart of the city stands the Grand Bazaar, a vast covered market—a veritable city within a city—around which you could wander for days. Although parts of the market specialize in selling souvenirs to tourists, do not be deceived: the bazaar is still a functioning market, producing a huge range of wares in its workshops, and patronized by the locals to purchase everything from carpets and furnishings to leatherwear and jewelry. Other shopping opportunities in Istanbul include the Spice Bazaar, and flea markets, as well as many Western-style shopping areas with boutiques and malls.

Inspired by Byzantine architecture, the domes and minarets of Ottoman mosques dominate the Istanbul skyline.

SAILING TO BYZANTIUM

Istanbul, which means "The City," has a long and glorious history. Legend holds that it was founded by Bizas; hence its original name, Byzantium. For a thousand years, it was a small Greek trading colony, but in 324 C.E. the first Christian emperor, Constantine the Great (c. 274–327 C.E.), chose it to be the new capital of the Roman Empire, renaming it Constantinople. The city was a beacon of culture through the European Dark Ages, but by the fifteenth century, its strength was exhausted. In 1453 it fell to Mehmet II, and for the next four-and-a-half centuries was reborn as the capital of the Ottoman Empire.

WHAT TO DO

* With some 3,600 shops and 61 streets, the labyrinthine Grand Bazaar (Kapali Carsi) is guaranteed to keep the most dedicated shopper busy. Originally laid out according to different wares and crafts (carpet makers, goldsmiths, etc), the bazaar is a place to find Turkish crafts: hand-painted ceramics, carpets, and brassware; gold jewelry; textiles, and clothing, including inexpensive leather and suede goods; antiques, decorative items, and souvenirs. A selection of restaurants and cafés provide convenient refueling stations, and a chance to consult your map of the bazaar, while reviving yourself with a cup of thick black Turkish coffee.

* The Grand Bazaar is only one of the city's traditional shopping spaces. Another market worth a visit, and a place to taste the many varieties of *lokum*, Turkish delight candy, is the Spice Bazaar (Misir Carsisi). You can also purchase a range of Turkish wares at the Sanatlari Carsisi (Bazaar of Istanbul Arts), the Caferaga Medrese, and in the Arasta (old bazaar) of the Sultanahmet Mosque.

* Not far from the Grand Bazaar on Beyazit Meydani (Beyazit Square), the city's largest flea market takes place every Sunday. Wander through the stalls, carts, or piles of bric-a-brac laid out on mats on the street, and you never know what treasure you might find. Nearby is the Old Book Bazaar (Sahaflar Carsisi), which sells mainly Turkish- and Arabic-language books, but which is a must for the bibliophile. Other flea markets can be found around the city and its suburbs, in Topkapi (Sultan's palace) district, on Cukurcuma Sokak in Cihangir, and Buyuk Hamam Sokak in Uskudar.

* Istanbul has more to offer than medieval bazaars and colorful flea markets. Fashionable boutiques can be found in the area around Taksim Square, the heart of the modern city of Istanbul. And there are several major shopping malls, including the Galleria, Carousel, Capitol, Polcenter, and Akmerkez, which has won the Best European Shopping Center Award twice in 1995 and 1998.

WHEN TO VISIT

Istanbul benefits from the mild Mediterranean climate, and the summer heat is tempered by ocean breezes. Like much of southern Europe, the best times of year to visit the city are spring (April–May) and fall (September–October). Summer will attract crowds of visitors, and the winter can be gray and damp with high rainfall.

The aromatic wares of Misisr Carisi, the spice bazaar, create a heady mixture of sight and smells for the shopper used to the sealed packaged goods of Western supermarkets.

THE TURKISH BATH (*HAMAM*)

Inheritors of the public bathing traditions of the Roman and Byzantine empires, the Turks developed their own version, the *hamam*. Apart from a place to get clean, the *hamam* is a place in which to relax and socialize. Once inside the section assigned to your sex (the *hamam* is a very respectable environment), you change in a private cubicle in the *camekan*. When you have traded your clothes for a towel, you enter the *sogukluk*, or cooling-off room, before going to the marble *hararet*, the hot or steam room. The center of the room is occupied by a heated domed marble platform, the *gobek tasi*, on which bathers can receive a vigorous massage and skin scrub or just relax. You return to the *camekan* to rest, chat, and change. Neighborhood *hamams* are fast disappearing, replaced by home bathing facilities, but several historical baths have been preserved in Istanbul. The oldest is the sixteenth-century domed Cemberlitas Hamamı, located close to the Grand Bazaar, a great place to recuperate after a busy day's bargain hunting. Other historic Istanbul *hamams* include the Galatasaray Hamam in Beyoglu and Cagaloglu Hamam in Sultanahmet.

References & Resources

Recommended Reading, Listening, and Viewing (●) Normally, reference sections recommend books and web sites, but for some trips, I have also recommended several audio CDs and DVDs. Bookwise, there are many excellent travel guides that give readers all they need to know about the practical aspects of traveling to different destinations. These include the Baedeker, Fodor, Lonely Planet, Rough Guides, and Blue Guides. Rather than recommending a specific guidebook for each trip, I have suggested books that will give you an insight into the country or city you might be visiting.

Internet sites (✴) A great deal of information is now available online, from national tourist organizations (NTOs), travel companies, business sites, and guidebook publishers. Because of the fast-changing nature of the Internet, I have listed mainly the principal NTO web sites, as these are likely to remain, as well as the sites of specific establishments or events listed in the book. However, as the listing is not meant to be comprehensive, it is always worth going online, typing your destination into a search engine, and seeing what comes up. A tip for searching online is to be as precise as possible. Type in "England" or "France" and you will get millions of hits, but type in "Royal National Theatre+London" or "Louvre Museum+Paris," and you will get a much more focused list of web sites.

General travel

✴ www.who.int
For vaccination advice and up-to-date health information for all areas

✴ www.lonelyplanet.com
The web site of the travel guide publisher giving basic information on every country, as well as a forum for travelers to swap tips

✴ www.roughguides.com
Another leading travel guide publisher's web offering with useful worldwide information

✴ www.fodors.com
The site for the Fodor guides

✴ www.travel.state.gov
Advice for travelers from the U.S. State Department

✴ www.fco.gov.uk
Advice for travelers from the U.K. government

Australia

✴ www.deh.gov.au

✴ www.atn.com.au

● Hill, B [1995] The Rock: Travelling to Uluru, Allen and Unwin

● Arnold, C. and Arnold, P. [2003] Uluru: Australia's Aboriginal Heart, Clarion Books

Austria

✴ www2.salzburg.info

✴ www.aboutaustria.org

● Gutman, R. [2000] Mozart: A Cultural Biography, Harcourt

● Steinberg, M. [2000] Austria as Theater and Ideology: The Meaning of the Salzburg Festival, Cornell University Press

● Vienna Waltz [1995] Audio CD Johann II Strauss

Belize

✴ www.travelbelize.org

● Wright, R. [2000] Travels Among the Maya: Travels in Belize, Guatemala and Mexico, Grove Press

Cambodia

✴ www.tourismcambodia.com

● Fay, K. and Fay, J [2004] To Asia with Love: A Connoisseurs' Guide to Cambodia, Laos, Thailand and Vietnam, Global Directions Inc/Things Asian Press

Dubai

✴ www.dubaicityguide.com

● Sampler, J. and Elgner, S. [2003] Sand to Silicon: Achieving Rapid Growth Lesson from Dubai, Profile Business

Ecuador

* ✳ www.galapagos.com
* ✳ www.galapagosislands.com
* ✳ www.darwinfoundation.org
* ● Fitter, J., Fitter, D. and Hosking, D. [2002] *Wildlife of the Galapagos*, Princeton University Press

France

* ✳ www.francetourism.com
* ✳ www.francebalade.com
* ✳ www.chateauxloire.com
* ✳ www.milaudiere.com
* ✳ www.ville-orleans.fr
* ✳ www.ecole.vins-bordeaux.fr
* ✳ www.bordeaux-tourisme.com
* ✳ www.modeaparis.com
* ✳ www.discoverfrance.net
* ✳ www.parisdigest.com
* ✳ www.galerieslafayette.com
* ● Droste, T. and Mosler, A. [1997] *The Chateaux of the Loire*, I.B. Tauris
* ● Parker, R. [2003] *Bordeaux: A Consumer's Guide to the World's Finest Wines*, Simon & Schuster
* ● *Prêt-à-Porter* [1994] DVD Dir. Robert Altman

Greece

* ✳ www.gnto.gr
* ✳ www.knossos.gr
* ● MacGillivray, J. [2000] *Minotaur: Sir Arthur Evans and the Archaeology of the Minoan Myth*, Hill & Wang

Guatemala

* ✳ www.terra.com.gt/turismogt
* ✳ www.tikalpark.com
* ● Wright, R. [2000] *Travels Among the Maya: Travels in Belize, Guatemala and Mexico*, Grove Press

Hong Kong

* ✳ www.discoverhongkong.com
* ● O'Reilly, J., Habegger, L. and O'Reilly (eds) [1996] *Traveler's Tales: Hong Kong*, Traveler's Tales Guides

Iceland

* ✳ www.icetourist.is
* ● Scudder, B. [1998] *Iceland: Life and Nature on a North Atlantic Island*, Iceland Review

India

* ✳ www.india-tourism.net/Palaceonwheels.htm
* ✳ www.beachandlakeresort.com
* ✳ www.shantibhavanyoga.com
* ✳ www.keralatourism.org
* ● Chaline, E. [2002] *Simple Path to Yoga*, Barnes and Noble Books
* ● Keay, J. [2001] *India: A History*, Grove Press
* ● Theroux, P. [1995] *The Great Railway Bazaar*, Penguin Books

Italy

* ✳ www.italiantourism.com
* ✳ www.it-schools.com/sections/italian-cooking-schools-in-italy/sicilyc/index.shtml
* ✳ www.carnivalofvenice.com
* ✳ www.casagrugno.it
* ✳ www.cucinadelsole.it
* ✳ www.cameramoda.it
* ✳ www.milano24ore.net
* ✳ www.lifeinitaly.com
* ● Adams, L. [2001] *Italian Renaissance Art*, Westview Press
* ● Tasca Lanza, A. [1996] *The Flavors of Sicily: Stories, Traditions, and Recipes for Warm-Weather Cooking*, Clarkson Potter
* ● Norwich, J. [1989] *A History of Venice*, Vintage
* ● *Prêt-à-Porter* [1994] DVD Dir. Robert Altman

Japan

* ✳ www.jnto.go.jp
* ✳ www.kyoto-izusen.com
* ● Mosher, Gouverneur [1985] *Kyoto: A Contemplative Guide*, Tuttle and Co.
* ● Chaline, E. [2003] *The Book of Zen: Path to Inner Peace*, Barron's Educational Series

Laos

* www.visit-laos.com
● Fay, K. and Fay, J. [2004] *To Asia with Love: A Connoisseurs' Guide to Cambodia, Laos, Thailand and Vietnam*, Global Directions Inc/ Things Asian Press

Mexico

* www.visitmexico.com
● Wright, R. [2000] *Travels Among the Maya: Travels in Belize, Guatemala and Mexico*, Grove Press

New Zealand

* www.newzealand.com
● Molloy, L. [1994] *Wild New Zealand*, MIT Press

Romania

* www.turism.ro
* www.romaniatourism.com
● Treptow, K. [2000] *Vlad III Dracula: The Life and Times of the Historical Dracula*, Center for Romanian Studies

Russia

* www.russia-travel.com
* www.petersburgcity.com
* www.waytorussia.net
● Volkov, Solomon [1995] *Petersburg: A Cultural History*, New York and London, Free Press

Singapore

* www.visitsingapore.com
* www.expatsingapore.com
● Turnbull, C. [1989] *A History of Singapore*, 1819-1988, Oxford University Press

South Africa

* www.southafrica.net
* www.SANParks.org
● Kruger, K. [2001] *The Wilderness Family: At Home with Africa's Wildlife*, Ballantine

Thailand

* www.chiangmai.com
* www.thailand.com/travel
* www.chiangmai-online.com/ thai-kitchen
* www.chiangmaiinfo.com
● McDermott, N. [1992] *Real Thai: The Best of Thailand's Regional Cooking*, Chronicle Books

The Netherlands

* www.holland.com
● Dash, M. [2001] *Tulipomania : The Story of the World's Most Coveted Flower & the Extraordinary Passions It Aroused*, Three Rivers Press

Turkey

* www.tourismturkey.org
* www.istanbultravelguide.net
* www.cemberlitashamami.com.tr
● Norwich, J. [1998] *A Short History of Byzantium*, Vintage

United Kingdom

* www.nt-online.org
* www.stratford-upon-avon.co.uk
* www.shakespeares-globe.org
* www.londontheatre.co.uk
* www.timeout.com
* www.whatsoninlondon.co.uk
* www.english-heritage.org.uk
* www.visitbritain.com
* www.glastonburytor.org.uk
● Ackroyd, P. [2003] *London: The Biography*, Anchor
● Chippendale, C. [2004] *Stonehenge Complete*, Thames and Hudson
● Mann, N. [2001] *The Isle of Avalon: Sacred Mysteries of Arthur and Glastonbury*

United States of America

* www.travelalaska.com
● *Alaska: Spirit of the Wild* [1999] DVD narrated by Charlton Heston

Vietnam

* www.vietnamtourism.com
● Fay, K. and Fay, J. [2004] *To Asia with Love: A Connoisseurs' Guide to Cambodia, Laos, Thailand, and Vietnam*, Global Directions Inc/Things Asian Press

Experience Index

To enable you to create the perfect combination of romance, adventure, activity, gastronomy, culture, spirituality, and shopping on your next vacation, I have organized the destinations, excursions, and events described in each trip into an easy-to-use index.

ROMANTIC

Aurora Borealis, Alaska **67**
Chateau d'Azay-le-Rideau,
    France **28, 30**
Chateau de Chenonceau, France **31**
Dalat, Vietnam **70**
Viennese Fasching **84**
Fatehpur Sikri, India **25, 26**
Jag Niwas, Udaipur, India **27**
Jaipur, India **26, 27**
Red Arrow Express, Russia **17**
Taj Mahal, India **24, 25, 26**
Venice Carnevale **20–3**

ACTIVE

Aalsmeer and Flora Holland flower
    auctions **39**
Blue Lagoon, Iceland **52, 53**
Bollenstreek Corso, Holland **39**
Cemberlitas Hamamı, Turkey **139**
Doi Inthanon Park, Thailand **112**
Hakone, Japan **100**
Hamam, Turkey **139**
Hanmer Springs and
    Maruia Springs, New Zealand **58**
Husavik, Iceland **52**
Jumeirah Park, Dubai **127**
Kgalagadi Transfrontier Park and
    Kruger National Park, South
    Africa **36**
Lighthouse Beach, India **90**
Mae Sa Elephant Camp,
    Thailand **112**
Naad Al Sheba Race Course,
    Dubai **127**
Nha Trang, Vietnam **71**
Queenstown, New Zealand **59**
Sinaia, Romania **48**
Wolf, Darwin Isabela islands,
    Galapagos **44, 45**

OFF-TRACK

Aoraki Mount Cook,
    New Zealand **59**
Calakmul Rainforest Biosphere,
    Central America **61, 62**
Denali National Park, Alaska **65, 66**
Drakensberg Mountains, South
    Africa **36**
Fagaras Mountains, Romania **48**
Franz Joseph and Fox glaciers,
    New Zealand **59**
Geysir and Strokkur, Iceland **52**
Gullfloss, Iceland **52**
Halong Bay, Vietnam **71**
Helgafell, Iceland **52**
Keukenhof Gardens, Holland **39**
Kenai Peninsula, Alaska **65, 66**
Lake Myvatn, Iceland **52**
Lake Wanaka, New Zealand **59**
Periyar Wildlife Sanctuary, India **90**
Poienari Castle, Romania **48**
Pushkar, India **27**
Samaria Gorge, Crete **81**
Sapa, Vietnam **71**
Snaefellsjokull, Iceland **52**
Table Mountain, South Africa **37**
The Wilderness National Park,
    South Africa **37**

CULTURAL

Angkor Thom, Ta Prohm,
and Angkor Wat, Vietnam **69, 70**
Arena di Verona, Italy **22**
Brasov, Romania **48**
Chateau de Chambord, France **30**
Copan, Central America **61, 63**
Gion, Japan **120, 121**
Globe Theatre, London **74, 76, 77**
Hermitage Museum, Russia **18**
Hue, Vietnam **71**
Knossos, Phaistos,
Malia, and Zarkos, Crete **78–81**
Lamanai, Central America **63**
Mariinsky (Formerly Kirov) Theater,
Russia **18**
Orléans, France **30**
Palio di Sienna, Italy **23**
Petrodvorets, Russia **19**
Royal National Theatre,
London **74, 76**
Salzburger Festspiele, Austria **85**
San Gimignano, Italy **23**
Santorini, Greece **78, 81**
Schönbrunn Castle, Austria **84**
Sighisoara and Sibiu, Romania **48**
Stratford-upon-Avon, England **77**
Tikal, Central America **61, 62**
Tsarkoe Selo, Russia **19**
West End, London **74, 75, 76**
Wiener Festwochen, Austria **85**

SPIRITUAL

Avesbury and West Kennet
Long Barrow, England **98**
Beach and Lake Resort, Trivandrum,
India **89, 90**
Glastonbury, England **96-99**
Helgafell, Iceland **52**
Kata Tjuta, Australia **93, 95**
Luang Prabang and
Pak Ou Caves, Vietnam **70, 71**
Mount Fuji, Japan **100-3**
Shanti Bhavan, India **90**
Shivananda Yoga Ashram, India **90**
Stonehenge, England **96–9**
Tjukurpa, Australia **93, 95**
Uluru, Australia **92–95**
Wat Phra Borommathat
Temple, Thailand **112**

GASTRONOMIC

Bourg and Blaye, France **108**
Catania, Sicily **115**
Chiang Mai, Thailand **110–3**
Daiji-in, Japan **120**
Dviranskoye Gnezdo, Russia **18**
Entre-Deux-Mers, France **107, 108**
Graves and Medoc, France **107, 108**
Sadya, India **91**
Sannenzaka and Ninenzaka,
Japan **120**
Saint-Emilion, Pomerol,
and Fronsac, France **107, 108**
Taormina, Sicily **114–6**
Viagrande, Sicily **116**
Wines of the Val de Loire,
France **28–31**

CONSUMER

Arab Street, Chinatown,
and Little India, Hong Kong **135**
Beyazit Meydani flea market
and Sahaflar Carsisi, Turkey **137–8**
Boulevard Haussman, France **130**
Dubai Shopping Festival **126**
Faubourg Saint-Honoré
and the Avenue Montaigne,
France **130**
Galleria Vittorio Emanuele,
Italy **128, 129**
Gold Souk, Dubai **126**
Great Singapore Sale **133**
Hanoi, Vietnam **70**
Kapali Carsi, Turkey **138**
Kovalam, India **90**
Li Yuen Street East and West,
Hong Kong **134**
Misir Carsisi, Turkey **138**
Meena Bazaar, Dubai **127**
Nevsky Prospekt, Russia **18**
Orchard Road, Singapore **135**
Pacific Place, Hong Kong **134**
Rue de la Paix, France **130**
Taksim Square, Turkey **138**
Via Montenapoleone, Italy **131**
Yau Ma Tai Jade Market,
Hong Kong **134**